FLOOR DEALERS CAN
BEAT THE BOXES
AND ESCAPE THE
CHEAP-PRICE RAT RACE
OF DOOM FOREVER

....

THE ULTIMATE *"UNFAIR ADVANTAGE"*
GUIDE FOR
DOUBLING YOUR PROFITS,
DOMINATING YOUR PROFITS,
BUILDING YOUR *IDEAL LIFESTYLE*, AND
HAVING FUN MAKING THE
BOX STORES EAT YOUR DUST!

JIM AUGUSTUS ARMSTRONG

CreateSpace
Charleston, SC

Flooring Success Systems
236 South 3rd St., Suite 309
Montrose, CO 81401
1-877-887-5791
Support@FlooringSuccessSystems.com

Book Layout ©2013 BookDesignTemplates.com

Image Copyright:
Face palm man: durantelallera/Shutterstock
Rattle snake: anton_novik/Shutterstock

Ordering Information:
For information on quantity purchases by corporations, associations, and others, contact the publisher at the address, email or phone number above.

How Floor Dealers Can Beat The Boxes And Escape The Cheap-Price Rat Race Of Doom Forever; The Ultimate Guide For Doubling Your Profits, Dominating Your Market, Building Your *Ideal Business*, Living Your *Ideal Lifestyle*, And Having Fun Making Competitors Eat Your Dust
By Jim Augustus Armstrong. -- 2nd ed.
ISBN: 9781792063527

CONTENTS

ACKNOWLEDGEMENTS

....

I started my first business when I was in 8th grade. Since then I have owned a number of businesses and done a tremendous amount of selling. During that time, so many people have added to my business knowledge and provided support and inspiration that listing them all would be impossible. However, I want to mention several people who have been great resources and supporters:

Dustin Aaronson, Steve Feldman and the rest of the team at Floor Covering News for their continued support and friendship over the years. Robert Skrob for his invaluable business and marketing guidance. Bruce Glines for his ongoing support, friendship and invaluable insights. Tracy Tolleson for his tremendous help and inspiration when I launched *Flooring Success Systems* in 2007. Susan Trainor for her insightful, quality editing. Tiffany Hoeckelman for her excellent cover design. Rich Selby for his ongoing input and guidance. Mom and Dad for instilling a distaste for traditional employment at a young age, thereby helping ensure I would forever be an entrepreneur. (AKA "unemployable.") Dan Kennedy and Joe Polish: their educational materials first introduced me to the fundamental differences between "traditional advertising" and "direct response marketing." Their no-nonsense, results-oriented approach to marketing has been a huge inspiration.

Bobbie Cooper for her support and belief in the beginning. (Thanks, Lett. I'll never forget it.)

Finally, I want to mention my business partner and biggest source of inspiration and encouragement: my amazing wife, Jolyn. In this

1

space I can't possibly do justice to all she does to make our businesses and our lives incredible. So I'll just say, "Thank you for all you do, Hon."

QUIZ TO DETERMINE IF YOU
SHOULD READ THIS BOOK

....

You might be wondering if reading this book is going to be a waste of time; if it will even apply to your business. Well, I certainly don't want you to waste your time—you're busy! You might even be working 50-70 hours per week, including weekends, like a lot of dealers before they learned the strategies in this book. So I've developed a quiz to help you decide if this is the right book for you. Tell me ...

Which of these "dramas" sound familiar? Check all that apply.

❑ **You lose another sale because you can't match Home Depot's "Free Installation."** You know it's a big lie; that Home Depot marks up their products to make up the difference. But try telling that to your customers when they've got "free" on the brain.

❑ **You spend $8,000 on a full color newspaper circular** and the only response you get is from a lady who wants vinyl for a tiny bathroom in her rental. After she blows an hour of your time having you haul out samples and giving her prices, she says she's going to "check around" and get back to you.

❑ **You lose yet another sale to a flooring installer who sells products out of his truck at "cost" just to get the installation work.**

❑ **You see a customer and her best friend at Starbucks,** and it turns out the best friend just installed flooring from Lumber

3

Liquidators. The friend didn't refer you ... she didn't even tell her *best friend* about you.

- **For you there's no such thing as "weekend"** ... one work-week just blends into another.

- **You drive by your competitor's store and you get that queasy feeling because their parking lot is packed full of cars.** Then you notice that one of the cars belongs to someone you *thought* was a loyal past customer. You reach for the Alka-Seltzer.

- **You've been working with a distributor for years.** You thought they were on your side. One day you find out they are selling directly to the public and undercutting your prices.

- **You've been working 50, 60, 70 hours a week** for so long that you have to pull up photos on your smartphone to remind yourself what your kids look like.

- **You're backing out of your driveway, on your way to another 12-hour grind,** and you see your competitor's installation van parked in front of a neighbor's house. You have to fight the urge to pull back into the driveway and go back to bed.

- **It's Saturday and you're missing your daughter's soccer game (again) because you have to work.**

- **You pay a lead service $1,200** and all you get are two bottom feeders who want you to cut, cut, cut your prices until your margins are lying on the ground in tatters. So you cave on price to "get the sale," and how do they repay you? By complaining and nit-picking through the entire project and giving you ulcers.

- **How does it feel when yet another prospect walks into your showroom wanting you to slash your prices until you bleed?** So you do, but they buy from your competitor anyway because he's willing to slash until he's losing money just to "keep his installers busy."

❑ **Your customer asks "How much is this?"** and your ulcer flares up because they told you they were just at Home Depot looking at the same product, and there's no way you can match their price. You've just lost another sale before you've even gotten to bid on it!

❑ **Your spouse files a missing person report with the police because your family hasn't seen you in weeks.**

❑ **You walk through your showroom and overhear a customer telling your salesperson they can get their 3,500 sq. ft. home re-carpeted cheaper at Home Depot.** He doesn't know what to say. He doesn't overcome their objection. He manages to stammer something about "getting what you pay for." An hour later the customer leaves without buying. How does it feel watching $6,000 walk out the door for Home Depot because your salesperson sucks at selling?

❑ **Your last vacation was your honeymoon.**

❑ **You walk into your break room and your two sales team members are back there reading magazines ...** because there's not a customer to be seen anywhere in your showroom. And there hasn't been for two days because Home Depot is having yet another "blowout" flooring sale.

❑ **It's the middle of another sleepless night,** you're lying in a pool of your own sweat, staring at the ceiling, wondering if it's all worth it. **OR ...**

❑ **You're an already-successful dealer, and you're open-minded about learning new strategies that can help you be even *more* successful.**

If any of these sound familiar, then this book is just for you. If you know deep down that something's gotta give; that you want transformational change for your business; that you deserve to make a lot *more* money (I'm talking millions more) with a lot less stress; that it's time you had the freedom to enjoy life—then you're in the right place. The proven methods I teach in this book will work for you, no matter how big or how small your company. No matter what market you're in.

Since 2007, I've worked with hundreds of flooring dealers, helping them to transform their businesses, make more money than they ever thought possible, and (most importantly) gain the time and freedom to live their *Ideal Lifestyle*. Here are just a few of the dealers you're going to meet in this book, and the amazing results they've gotten by using the proven strategies you're going to learn:

Tim Rea from Minnesota was throwing away $15,000 - $20,000 per month on "traditional" advertising that wasn't working. After using my proven methods for less than three months, he completely stopped advertising and his sales went up. He pocketed that extra $15k - $20k each month.

Dan Ginnaty from Montana felt like a slave to his store, working too many hours, no vacations. That's all changed. I showed him how to let his store work for him instead of the other way around. He recently returned from a vacation to Costa Rica with his wife. He also replaced ALL of his "traditional" advertising with a single marketing strategy (that you'll learn about in this book), and now attracts a much higher quality customer, willing to pay his prices. (His residential margins are at 45%.) Not to mention all the money he's saved since he stopped throwing it away on ineffective advertising.

Jimmy Williams from North Carolina now tells "price shoppers" that he's the "most expensive store in the county," and he still gets the sale.

Steve D'Angelo from Arizona was discouraged with results he was getting from "traditional" advertising. After 24 months of applying my proven methods, his sales tripled. In fact, a lot of competitors in his area went out of business during the "Great Recession" that began in 2008. Steve has scooped up all that business. He's literally the "last man standing."

Dean from South Carolina was taking a personal salary of over $400,000, but he was working 60-70 hours per week, and was rarely able to spend time with his daughters. He was a "successful slave." After less than one month of working with me, I showed him how to free up an entire day a week. In that first year he took his girls on a vacation to Disney World. He has learned how to make his store work for *him*.

All these stories (and the others you'll read about in this book) happened during what's described as the worst U.S. economy since the Great Depression. And there are many, many more success stories like these. Dealers who were desperate, miserable — some broke, some making a ton of money — they all had one thing in common: They knew they wanted transformational change in their businesses and their lives. And they used my proven methods to make it happen. Now they are successful, happy, making more money than ever before, and they have fulfilling lives with plenty of money and freedom to do all the things they enjoy *outside* of business. They've learned how to make their flooring business work for THEM instead of the other way around.

*You've probably noticed that I keep using the word proven.

That's because the strategies I'm going to reveal to you in this book have been proven to work by hundreds of flooring dealers. I have dealers with a single location, multiple locations, even mobile showrooms. Some are in big cities, some way out in the boondocks, and everywhere in between. Coast-to-coast, all across the U.S. and Canada, my dealers are exploding their profits and smoking their competition!

I want you to meet one of those dealers right now.

Meet Mark Bouquet, A Fellow Flooring Dealer Who Not Long Ago Was Thinking, "Maybe Shutting My Doors Is My Best Option," But Recently Did Over $3 Million, And Now Has Less Stress And The Freedom He Imagined When He Started His Business!

Mark Bouquet was not always a flooring marketing and advertising expert, and certainly not as successful as he is today. In fact far, far from it. Actually, he was on the verge of shutting the doors of his flooring business in Illinois not too long ago.

I remember the day when he decided enough was enough. It was Wednesday, October 23, 2008, when I got a phone call from Mark. He was desperate, and the reason why will become very clear in a moment.

Think back to fall 2008. Do you remember what happened? The United States was on the verge of the largest financial meltdown since the Great Depression, and the U.S. government and the public were in a panic. We were also in the midst of a total collapse of the housing market; home prices were plummeting, banks had stopped lending, and foreclosures were becoming epidemic. Remember that? Well, it was right in the middle of this crisis that Mark called me, and here is what he told me:

His flooring business was 80% new construction. The housing boom of the early 2000's had been a huge blessing for Mark, but when the housing market collapsed it turned into a curse. Here Mark was with 80% of his business coming from new construction, when virtually overnight people *stopped buying houses*! And to make matters much, much worse, because of all the foreclosures and abandoned properties, Mark's county had put a moratorium on new building permits. This meant no one was allowed to build new homes in his county.

And If All That Wasn't Bad Enough ...

Mark suffered from some serious health issues that kept him out of his store most days. His wife and son were running the store when he was out.

In Summary: Mark's business was 80% new construction, his county stopped allowing any new housing construction, and he suffered from health issues that kept him away from the store. That's when he called me. And he had just one question:

Could my methods turn things around for him before it was too late? I told him "yes," but there was no time to lose. He immediately began implementing the strategies I teach.

Fast forward 6 months ...

I got another phone call from Mark, but this time the news was much different. He sounded super excited over the phone, and he couldn't wait to give me the good news! He told me his business was now almost 100% residential remodel (no more dependence on new construction), his installations were booked out for six weeks, and he was having to find new installers just to keep up with all the new sales! Plus his margins were at 40% or more! He was not having to resort to "cheap-price" advertising to get business! All as a result of using primarily one of the marketing strategies you'll learn about in this book.

Here's a note Mark sent me:

"Jim ... our business is growing exponentially. There is no comparison between my company now and before I joined *Flooring Success Systems*. I can't believe the turnaround here! October was our busiest month in 20 years. November was our second busiest month. And this month (July) we are crashing new records!"

And It Gets Even Better: In 2013 Mark Did Over $3 Million In Sales!

And this after nearly going out of business not long before. Have you ever heard the saying, *When the student is ready the teacher will appear?* Well, that is what I believe happened with Mark. And it can happen with you, too, if you are open to new ways of doing business.

My ongoing surveys of dealers across North America reveal that traditional advertising does not work. Even so, most dealers continue throwing money away on it because they simply do not know any other way.

This book is about giving dealers another way.

With that in mind, you may encounter strategies and principles that are foreign or uncomfortable to you. That's because they are new; outside the norm; unconventional; not what everyone else is doing. Which is in large part why they work. If all I do is regurgitate the strategies that are failing legions of floor dealers, or tell you a bunch of things you already know, how does that help you? It doesn't. So expect the unexpected. Keep an open mind. And I promise that the time you spend reading this book will be the most profitable of your year ... possibly your entire career.

ICONS

....

Case Study
This icon means you're about to read a case study involving a real, live floor dealer using one or more of the strategies taught in this book.

Rule breaker!
This icon means you're about to get tips and strategies that break commonly followed "rules" of the flooring industry. Pay special attention because breaking these rules will help you get an *Unfair Advantage* over competitors, beat the boxes, and dramatically increase your profits!

Watch out!
This icon means you're about to be warned of a deadly pitfall that can hurt your profitability or success.

What the ...?
This icon means that Jim is about to discuss a commonly held flooring industry idea or belief that's so dumb or harmful to dealers that he gets severely torqued off even thinking about it.

JIM'S LEXICON

....

3 Tiers of Marketing. A method of prioritizing your marketing and advertising to maximize effectiveness and create the Marketing Multiplier effect.

5/45 Business. A dealership that does $5 million or more in gross revenue annually, with gross margins of 45% or more on residential flooring.

5/45 Dealer. A dealer who builds a $5 million business with gross margins of 45% or more on residential flooring.

Advertising By The Seat Of Your Pants. Reactive advertising. The opposite of "Marketing System." Having no overall marketing plan in place. Jumping at spur-of-the-moment pitches from ad reps selling newspaper space, embossed pens, radio ad space, etc., with no plan to prioritize, systemize, or track strategies that are implemented. This kind of advertising generates a lot of money ... for ad reps, not the floor dealer.

Brand Building. See "traditional advertising."

Bottom Feeder. A die-hard price shopper who does not care about quality, craftsmanship, customer service, or great warranties. Is only interested in beating you up on price until your margins are lying on the ground in bloody tatters. If you do land the sale by slashing your prices, God help you. They will reward you by complaining, nit-picking, and making your life hell throughout the entire project. Once you identify a bottom feeder, send them to your competition.

Direct Response Marketing. The kind of marketing I use and teach. The opposite of "traditional" or "brand building" advertising. It's designed to compel immediate response from your prospects and customers, create total differentiation, and make you the obvious choice. Uses benefits and unique selling propositions instead of product "features." It answers the unspoken question on every consumer's mind: Why should I do business with you instead of your competitor?

Ideal Business, Ideal Lifestyle™. Shorthand for my philosophy that the purpose of your business is to fund and facilitate your *Ideal Lifestyle*. I teach dealers how to build an *Ideal Business* that funds and facilitates their *Ideal Lifestyle*. It's also the name of my newsletter.

Little Rudders Steer Big Ships. Seemingly small changes in your approach to sales and marketing can create massive changes in your results.

Marketing System. A set of interconnected sales and marketing strategies working together to create the Marketing Multiplier effect, create differentiation, reduce price resistance and generate sales. Each strategy in a marketing system compounds the effectiveness of every other strategy. The whole is far more powerful than the sum of its parts.

Message, Market, and Media. Message is what you say. Market is who you say it to. Media is how the message is delivered. These function like legs on a three-legged stool. All are critical. If one is missing or weak, the whole thing collapses.

Name, Rank, And Serial Number Ads And Websites. Ads and websites that follow the following formula:

- Business name at the top
- Photos of products (sometimes with teaser prices)
- Contact information

The majority of flooring advertising follows this formula. The gigantic problem with these kinds of ads and websites is that they create no differentiation from your competitors. And when there's no differentiation, you wind up competing on price.

Purpose Of Your Business. To fund and facilitate your *Ideal Lifestyle.*

Traditional Advertising. Also known as "brand building" or "institutional advertising." It's the opposite of Direct Response Marketing. The basic idea is that you put your business name out there over and over again and hope that if enough people see your name enough times that you'll build up "name recognition," and that this will translate into sales. There's a tiny grain of truth to this. You can generate business this way. However there are three gigantic problems with it: 1) It's very slow; 2) there's a tremendous amount of waste; and 3) it's extremely expensive. Gigantic corporations (like box stores) can afford the time, money, and waste to make this work. Most floor dealers can't. Which is why I teach and use Direct Response Marketing strategies.

Unfair Advantage. This does not mean doing anything illegal or unethical. This means implementing unconventional strategies which (out of ignorance or laziness) most of your competitors won't. It means being willing to use strategies that ignore industry "norms." It describes a maverick attitude that says, "I don't care what everyone else is doing; I don't care what's popular; I don't care what the so-called 'experts' say; I demand big, measurable results from my marketing. Period." This combination of maverick attitude with an industry-defying approach to marketing gives dealers who adopt the strategies in this book a de facto *Unfair Advantage* over all competitors in their market place, including box stores.

Unspoken Question On Every Consumer's Mind. Every flooring consumer has an unspoken question on their mind: *Why should I do business with you instead of your competitors?* The vast majority of flooring advertising and websites do not answer this question, which is why many dealers wind up competing on price.

FREE OFFER

....

We've begun a new relationship with this book, and I don't want it to end when you reach the final page. As you read through each chapter, I think it will become obvious that there's a lot more to be gained from me that can fit within these pages. I'm also eager to help you put these strategies to work for you quickly.

For these reasons I'd like to offer you a complimentary *Dealership Diagnostic*. On the next page I've listed all the details and benefits of this service. My regular price for a *Dealership Diagnostic* is $500, but because you've ordered my book I'll give it to on a complimentary basis for a limited time.

Why not sign up for the *Dealership Diagnostic* right now while it's fresh on your mind? Yes, I'll remind you throughout the book, but the sooner you act the sooner you'll get the benefit of this service!

Complimentary 1-Hour Dealership Diagnostic

I'll personally give you a diagnostic of your market area to help you overcome the **"7 Deadly Problems,"** and to see if your business is a good candidate to **generate $5 Million/year with 45% margins or better**. Here's what we'll do during our hour together:

First, I'll ask you some questions about your business to help me understand **where you are at right now**, including:

- The population of your market area
- How many hours per week you're working vs. how many you'd like to work
- Advertising you're currently doing
- How much you're making vs. how much you'd like to make
- Who your biggest competitors are, etc.

Next we'll discuss where you **would like to be**.

- Increasing your income
- Eliminating the "feast or famine" cycles in your business
- Working less than 40 hours per week, no weekends, lots of vacations, etc.
- Having a stress-free business

Then I'll give you my best solutions for bridging the gap between **where you are and where you want to be.** I've done hundreds of Dealership Diagnostics, and most dealers have an "a-ha moment" when they see the solution to their problem right in front of them. You'll leave our meeting together with a game plan to overcome your problems and reach your goals! How awesome will THAT feel!

How To Secure Your Dealership Diagnostic...
Call us at 1-877-887-5791

A member of my team will schedule your appointment with me on the spot.

My normal fee for a Dealership Diagnostic is $500, but because you got my book I'll give it to you on a complimentary basis for a limited time.

Sales & Marketing Training For Your Organization

Are you a distributor, manufacturer, vendor, trade organization, trade show, or other organization serving the flooring industry? Jim can provide sales and marketing training for your group of flooring retailers, either in person or via webinar.

During Jim's trainings dealers learn how to **create total differentiation from their competitors, charge premium prices, and explode their profits in any market.** They also learn how to make their dealerships system-dependent rather than owner-dependent, thus enabling them to achieve higher levels of success, while at the same time having a fulfilling life outside their business.

The biggest strength about Jim's teaching method is that it's not textbook theory. Instead he gives dealers strategies he has been developing and using in his own businesses since 1993. They have been tested, tweaked, adjusted, and proven in hundreds real world flooring businesses from across the U.S. and Canada. Dealers walk away from Jim's sessions with actionable, nuts-and-bolts strategies they can use immediately to grow their revenues in the shortest time possible. The results speak for themselves. (See the dealer case studies in this book.)

Another strength Jim brings to the table is that, unlike many trainers hired for flooring events, he comes from inside the flooring industry. His business, Flooring Success Systems, is dedicated solely to serving floor dealers. His Marketing Mastery Column appears in every issue of Floor Covering News, he produces and co-hosts the monthly FCNews Marketing Mastery Webinars, and he's been a featured speaker at The International Surface Events.

For more information contact Flooring Success Systems at
1-877-887-5791

....

PART I

THE CORE 3
STRATEGIES

ONE

....

7 DEADLY PROBLEMS FACING FLOOR DEALERS TODAY

JIM: Is your advertising as effective as it was 10 years ago?

FLOOR DEALER: Not even close.

JIM: What are you doing differently to overcome this problem?

FLOOR DEALER: Uh …

Earlier you met Mark, the dealer from Illinois who nearly went out of business, but quickly turned things around using the methods I teach. Before meeting me, Mark faced 7 deadly problems in his flooring business. In fact, I've found that these problems are common to virtually all dealers. They will keep you permanently enslaved (even if you're making a lot of money), keep you struggling, even cause you to go out of business. If they don't force you to close your doors, they'll certainly cost you millions of dollars over the course of your career. These problems are only going to get worse in spite of an economy that's, as of this writing, somewhat healthier.

Deadly Problem #1:
The Only Thing Customers Care About Is Cheap Price

Here's a question I frequently ask dealers who attend my webinars and live speaking events: Are customers more price sensitive than 10 years ago? The overwhelming response is always "yes."

Home Depot, Lumber Liquidators, Lowe's, and other boxes and national discounters have brainwashed consumers into thinking that the only consideration when buying flooring is "Who is the cheapest?" Legions of dealers, in a desperate attempt to "compete," have followed suit. PROOF: I Googled "Flooring Los Angeles," and here is a screen shot of the search results ...

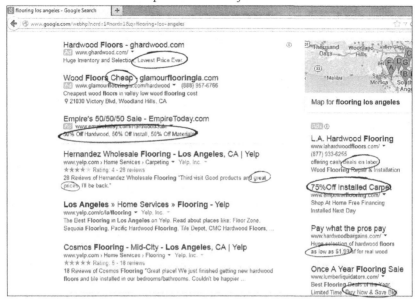

Every single flooring website at the top of the search results has "cheap-price" offers. Every *one of them*! Consumers are inundated with cheap-price offers. They're up to their eyeballs in them. They're drowning in them. Do you honestly believe that by putting out yet *another* low price offer—and cutting your margins to the bone—that you are going to stand out from your competitors and prosper in flooring retail? Do you think that dealers who do $5 million per year with 45%-50% margins are doing it with cheap-price come-ons, attracting bottom feeders? If you believe that, I've got a bridge in Brooklyn I want to sell you.

Does this sound familiar ...? You just did a bid for a new customer, she was super nice, you spent extra time on the estimate making sure you got everything just right. She assured you that she was going with you, but just needed to "confirm it with my husband." Three days later you see an installation van from your cheap-price competitor parked in front of her house. She didn't even call you! You know why? Because the minute you left her house she Googled "Flooring Cincinnati" (or whatever your city is) and found 20 of your competitors who were willing to do the same thing for less. This includes *Empire* and other online companies that don't even have a store in your area.

In fact, with the explosion of mobile devices, your customers are getting **instant** pricing from hundreds of competitors promising to do it cheaper than you. Heck, they're checking your prices against your competitors *right from your showroom*. (How does *that* make you feel?) This means that the downward price pressure on dealers is not going away. In fact, it's going to get a whole lot worse.

Deadly Problem #2:
Customer Loyalty Is Dead And Cremated, And The Ashes Are Sprinkled In Home Depot's Parking Lot.

How does it feel when you walk into a past customer's home because they need tile for their kitchen, but you notice they had someone else install hardwood throughout their entire home in the last three months? You didn't even know they were shopping for hardwood. How does it feel to miss out on a $10,000 sale that should have been yours?

Or how about when you need a plumbing fixture, so you go to Home Depot (because all the independent hardware stores in your town have been driven out of business) and you go to the flooring section (just to check it out) and you bump into one of your past customers talking to the flooring salesperson?

Or how about that customer with a bunch of rentals who used to send you business at least once a month, but you haven't heard from him in nearly a year? You hear through the grapevine that he now gets all his flooring online and pays a non-licensed contractor under the table to do the installations.

These kinds of stories happen to floor dealers *every day*. You used to be able to count on a certain level of customer loyalty. You did a good job, they repaid you by giving you repeat business and referrals. Period. It was dependable. It's how you built your business. You could count on it. Well, you can't count on *anything* anymore.

Your Customers Have Been Trained To Be Disloyal

Online, on TV, on the radio, in print, all they hear all day every day is "price, price, price, price, price." Doing a good job and providing good service is simply no longer enough to counter this onslaught. If you don't have a strategy in place specifically designed to counter the "cheap-price" brainwashing and keep your customers away from the competition, you can kiss those "loyal" customers good-bye ... in ever-increasing numbers.

Deadly Problem #3:
"Traditional" Advertising Doesn't Work

Another question I ask dealers on my webinars: *Is your advertising as effective as it was 10 years ago?* The overwhelming response is "NO!" In fact, these are the kinds of stories I hear every week from dealers about their advertising efforts. How many of these sound familiar?

- You get locked into a $4,000/month, year-long radio contract, and it generates no walk-in traffic. Literally zero walk-ins. You can't even pull the plug because you've got six more months to go on your contract. You would have been better off heaping that $4,000 into a pile each month, setting it on fire, and roasting marshmallows over it. At least that way you'd get some use out of it.

- You dump $5,000 on a full-page newspaper ad and you get two walk-ins. One of them wastes an hour looking at samples, but leaves when you won't sell her hardwood for $.99/ft. The other one tells you up front that she "doesn't want to spend a lot of money," and all she wants is your "lowest priced carpet." You show it to her, but she complains that it's still too expensive. So you cave and practically give the product away at the price she wants because you've got to cover the cost of your ad. And she still acts grumpy. She doesn't appreciate what you've done. Not even a "thank you." In fact, she complains throughout the project, demands last minute changes, and treats you like a criminal who will steal her blind if she's not careful. Your migraine flares up again.

- You spend 10 grand to send out 20,000 full-color mailers. All you get is a handful of walk-ins who turn out to be … yep, more bottom feeders who kick the tires, question your prices, and waste hours of your time.

Customers Obtained Through "Traditional" Advertising Don't Trust You

Here's another question I ask dealers during my live events: Are new customers more distrustful and skeptical than they were 10 years ago? The overwhelming answer is always "YES!"

Why the growing distrust …? Because your prospective customers have been lied to and ripped off by flooring companies, or they know someone who has. They've also been lied to and ripped off by politicians. By Wall Street. By internet scams. They've been spied on by their own government via the NSA. The financial meltdown and the collapse of the housing market in 2008 have left a permanent mindset of caution and fear.

Is it any wonder new customers who haven't bought from you before don't trust you? Why should they? As far as they know you could easily be another company out to lie to them and rip them off. But what if there was a way to use this fear, skepticism, and distrust to create customer *loyalty*? There is, and you'll learn how in this book.

Customers Don't Respect You

You may have been in the flooring business for decades. Maybe you took over the business from your parents. Your business has a good reputation. You're good at your craft. You really do take pride in your work. You deserve respect. But ...

- "Traditional" advertising attracts the worst of the worst customers ...
- Customers who don't respect you ...
- Who treat you with mistrust ...
- Who act like you're a criminal out to rip them off ...

It's as if they are coming into your store and spitting on your good name. Your *family's* name.

The good news is there are extremely profitable alternatives to "traditional" advertising. Strategies that attract only the best of the best. Customers who respect you. Who know the value of quality workmanship. Who are willing to pay a premium for your products.

Deadly Problem #4:
The Blind-And-Dumb Are Leading The Blind-And-Dumb

Dealers look at what the boxes are doing in their advertising, and then try to copy them. Then the other dealers copy *those* dealers. Until you have what we've got now: Everyone has ads and websites that say the exact same thing.

PROOF: How many floor dealer ads and websites have you seen that follow this formula:

- Business name at the top
- Photos of products (sometimes with teaser prices)
- Contact information

It's all you see! As I said earlier, I call these Name, Rank, and Serial Number ads and websites. (Maybe your website and ads follow this formula.) The gigantic problem with these kinds of ads and websites is that they create no differentiation from your competitors. And when there's no differentiation, how do your customers make a buying decision ...?

ON PRICE!

Dealers who build $5 million businesses with 45%-50% margins DON'T do it by copying all the other dealers. They create differentiation.

Does *Your* Advertising Answer The Unspoken Question On Every Prospective Customer's Mind?

Every one of your prospective customers who is searching online, or through the newspaper, or "shopping" local floor dealers has one burning question on their mind: *Why should I do business with you instead of your competitors?*

They are desperate for an answer to this question.

The bad news is that if you're using "traditional" advertising or *Name, Rank, and Serial Number* ads and websites, then you are *not* answering that question. You're not creating differentiation from your competitors. And you're *forcing* your customers to make their choice based on price.

Even So-Called Marketing "Experts" Copy The Copycats

I've heard industry experts suggest to dealers that they counter Home Depot's $39 installation by offering $29 installations, and then make up the difference by padding the cost of the materials. In other words, to play Home Depot's shell game. In other words, to lie. Now that Home Depot and others are offering "Free" installations, what are dealers supposed to do to beat that offer? Give rebates on installations?

Another reason this is disgusting is because it spits on the hard work and craftsmanship that go into a great installation. You and I know how critical the installation is. You can have the best product in the world and completely screw it up with a bad install. It treats installation like an afterthought. It devalues it. It trains consumers that high-quality installation by a skilled professional is only worth "$39." (Or worth nothing if you give it away free.)

These "experts" could give some very simple strategies for totally blowing away the "$39 Installation" lie (like I do for my dealers).

They could teach dealers strategies to build the value of installations in customers' minds. But they don't. They cave. They play the "cheap-price" game and teach other dealers to do the same. Unfortunately, too often this is what passes for marketing "training" in the flooring world.

Deadly Problem #5:
Costs Keep Going Up, But Margins Keep Going Down

To add injury to injury, all this downward price pressure is accompanied by a skyrocketing cost of doing business. Floor dealers are assaulted on all sides:

- Cost of goods going up
- Employee costs going through the roof
- Utilities going up
- Vehicle costs going up, especially fuel
- Higher insurance premiums

Not to mention the ever-increasing cost of living. Once you figure in increased food prices, utilities for your home, car insurance, health care, kids ... wow. And all these costs don't go away just because you have a "slow month." You gotta keep paying your employees, the utilities, insurance, rent, etc., even if you've got to pull money out of savings to do it. Dealers have a hangman's noose around their throats.

A Suicide Mission ...

In response to this crisis, many dealers try to sell more flooring by dropping their prices. They hope they'll make it up in volume. Dream on. You WON'T make it up in volume. This is a suicide mission that virtually guarantees you will either: 1) struggle forever; or 2) go belly up. (I detail why this is the case in an upcoming chapter.)

Deadly Problem #6:
Dealers Are Too Busy To Develop And Implement Effective Marketing Strategies

Dealers are pulled in 57 directions every day with all that goes in to running a flooring dealership—orders, estimates, managing employees, overseeing installers, tracking inventory. With most dealers already slaving away 50-70 hours per week ... *who has time to market???*

So dealers wind up copying each other by using the same old, tired, worn out, useless advertising they've always used. OR ... they do no marketing at all.

Deadly Problem #7:
The Feast-Or-Famine Cycle

Does this sound familiar? Business is slow, so you launch advertising campaigns and promotions, and work your tail off, hustling to get more business in your door. The next thing you know you're so swamped you can't keep up with the orders. So you stop doing the things that brought in the business because you're so busy running around putting out fires. You're stressed out, working nights and weekends. Your family never sees you. You wish for a break. The next thing you know your wish comes true. You get a nice, long break because your customers vanish like a burp in a breeze. Your showroom is as quiet as a graveyard at midnight. Panic sets in. Once again you launch promotions and start hustling to get new business.

And so it goes.

This is a common state of affairs for dealers because most have set up their businesses in such a way that they are forced to ride this nauseating up-and-down rollercoaster:

- They don't have an ongoing *marketing system* in place to create a steady stream of customers and even out the ups and downs, and bullet-proof their business against market downturns.

- They don't have a ***delegation system*** in place. When they get a spike in business, their *personal* workload spikes. They work longer hours, nights, weekends, and run around with their hair on fire trying to handle it all themselves. Until the spike turns into a dip. Then they panic from the lack of business.

Ironically, a rebounding economy makes this problem worse. Why? Because most dealers do not own their business; the business owns *them*. And this problem does not go away just because you generate millions in revenue. I worked with a dealer who did several million annually, and paid himself a personal salary of $400,000. But he worked 6-7 days a week, never took vacations, rarely got to spend time with his 2 daughters, and was totally burned out. In spite of a very good income, the business still owned *him*. Within 3 coaching calls I showed him how to reduce his workload to 40 hours per week or less, no weekends, and take time away from the business. That year he took his daughters on a vacation to Disney World in Florida.

In other words, to be a successful dealer with an *Ideal Business* and *Ideal Lifestyle*, generating more money is important, but it's only half of the recipe for success. You've got to have systems in place that create freedom and walkaway power for you so you can enjoy all that extra money! It's the difference between you owning your business, and your business owning <u>you.</u>

Dealers Are Failing To Capitalize On A Healthier Economy

For the same reasons listed above, very few dealers are poised to take advantage of a growing economy. As more orders come in their personal workload increases, and their lifestyle is sacrificed in a desperate attempt to keep up. What should be the good news of a somewhat healthier economy turns into the bad news of increased stress and more hours worked. Then when things inevitably slow down again, most dealers find themselves right back where they started. No permanent gain. A tempest in a teapot.

5/45 dealers capitalize on a growing economy — and seasonal spikes in business — to launch their business to an all new, **PERMANENT** level of success. And when sales increase, their workload actually decreases. They make more while working less.

Being "Good" Is No Longer Good Enough To Prosper And Thrive In Flooring

The real no-holds-barred, honest-to-goodness truth that few in the flooring industry want to admit, that 5/45 dealers will *never* tell you is this: It's *not* how much you know about flooring, or about having a huge line of quality products, or how good your location is, or how friendly your sales people are, or how nice and ethical a person you are.

The only solution is to learn the *Core 3* strategies for attracting a constant stream of high-paying customers that are happy to pay margins of 45%-50% (or more), and do it day-in and day-out, in any market, in any region of the country, and forever end the feast-or-famine cycle.

Just imagine having a day like this:

You drive to your beautiful new showroom that's on the corner of the busiest intersection in town. You have a big sign out front. Your parking lot is full of cars and your store is packed with customers.

You walk in at your usual time of 10:30 a.m. and look at the appointment calendar. It's packed with installations, all sold at 45%-50% margins. Your receptionist says that several customers visited this morning wanting to be "squeezed in." But they will have to be squeezed in two weeks from now. Your installers are already overbooked for the next two weeks.

The week after that is nearly filled up, too. What a great feeling! You can remember when this was your schedule for the whole month, not just a couple of days. You've got a few people to handle the business stuff and have excellent sales people handling the customers. These customers are perfectly happy paying full margin because your marketing attracts only the best of the best. Oh, and they're willing to wait in line for two weeks or more for their installation because they only want to work with you.

The feast-or-famine cycle doesn't happen anymore because it's <u>all feast</u>. Even when you get an onrush of new customers you don't panic because you have systems in place to handle all the new business. Your personal workload stays the same. No nights or weekends for you. You use the bump in sales as an opportunity to take your business to the next level. You've gone from being "self-employed" to being a true entrepreneur.

So what'll it be this afternoon—golf? The beach? Fishing? Hmmm???

CASE STUDY

How Jerome Raised His Margins From 30% to 50% And Stays Booked Out 6-12 Weeks!

Jerome Nowowiejski of Brownwood Decorating in Texas is one of my *Flooring Success Systems* members, and his story should be an inspiration to any dealer who is working too hard for too little, or who thinks that the *Ideal Business* and the *Ideal Lifestyle* I describe above are impossible for a floor dealer.

Jerome made an incredible transition in a short period of time, and since learning the strategies I teach, he has a better business as well as a better life. Before I met Jerome he had extremely low margins, between 18% and 30% on residential, yet within only three months of implementing the strategies he was learning from me, he began commanding margins between 45% and 50% on all his residential flooring.

Jerome has had his own flooring store since 2004. Before he put these new systems in place, he says the approach was, "Cat and mouse, scratching, trying to get everything you could"; he never left the store, was "worn out ... exhausted."

Jerome values the *Design Audit*™ for identifying the customers you maybe don't want to work with. "It weeds people out because you don't necessarily want to work with everybody," he says. "Perfect example: I had a lady who came in who just ripped me up one side and down the other on price. She came back in a year later ... this was after I had been introduced to Jim Armstrong and I started putting the systems in place. She started going through the same thing. So I said, 'I remember you, you're a returning customer. Let me sit down with you and ask you some questions' ... all her objections just dropped, and by the end of the conversation she was ready to move." That ended up being a $6,000-$7,000 job at over 40% margins. (*The Design Audit™* is my trademarked *Sales Closer System.* You'll learn more about this a little later.)

Jerome was once a slave to his store, working long hours and never taking weekends off. He now regularly takes four-day weekends, several multi-week vacations each year, even travelling out of the country. While he is away his business continues to run smoothly and make money. He says it's because of my strategies he has put in place: "That's what the *Design Audit*'s for, that's what all the mail-outs that we do before, during, and after the sale are for, that's what our checklist is for."

How's business now? Jerome is normally booked out for 2-3 months! He considers it "slow" when he's only booked out for 2 weeks. Why isn't he worried about telling customers they have to wait maybe three months for an installation? "Because most of my customers now are repeat business or referrals," he says. "They're not just coming in off the street." Jerome has also implemented strategies to create total differentiation from competitors, and he's implemented zero-resistance selling strategies. These combine to make prospects completely willing to wait weeks or months for their installation, even if a cheaper-priced competitor can do it that day. Most dealers would be terrified to tell a customer they had to wait three months; it's unthinkable. But that's because they have not implemented the strategies Jerome has. He now has total control over his business and his life. He owns his business, not the other way around.

Jerome now owns seven houses (some for rental income) and another on a lake nearby. All but one are paid off, and he owns his store and warehouse free and clear. Before joining

Flooring Success Systems he only had his own home and one rental property, both with mortgages. By investing the extra profits his business now generates into real estate, Jerome will likely have the option of early retirement if he chooses.

Jerome is proving every day that by implementing the strategies I teach, you can build your *Ideal Business* and live your *Ideal Lifestyle.*

Now that's what it's like to have fun being a floor dealer! If you have to drag yourself out of bed in the morning because you hate to go to work or if you're working like a dog early morning till late at night, you might as well go get a job working for someone else—heck, life's too short! Running your own business should be mentally, emotionally, and most of all financially rewarding, with plenty of time to take off to go out and enjoy life! You don't need to be a marketing expert to make these dreams a reality. All you need are the strategies I cover in this book.

TWO

....

THE THREE TIERS
OF MARKETING

JIM: How much are you spending on advertising?

FLOOR DEALER: $30,000 a year, all of it on radio, TV, and pay-per-click ads.

JIM: So you're spending a fortune trying to get strangers in your door, and totally ignoring the only people on the planet who have proven they will buy from you and send you referrals: your past customers.

FLOOR DEALER: Uh …

"Which marketing strategy should I start with?"

I was conducting a Q&A webinar for floor dealers, and one of the attendees asked this question. It's one I get asked a lot, and no wonder. There are hundreds of ways to promote your flooring business, both online and offline, and some of them require a substantial investment.

To make matters more confusing for dealers, every print ad rep, promotional gift item rep, web designer, radio and TV advertising rep, and SEO "expert" who mails, calls, or wanders into your store claims that you should start with whatever *they* happen to be selling. Many dealers wind up buying whatever gets suggested to them that day; in other words, marketing by the seat of their pants. It's easy to get overwhelmed by all the options and contradictory advice.

Here's a way to look at your marketing and advertising that will help narrow down the options, help you decide which strategies to begin with, and give you the biggest bang for your buck, and an *Unfair Advantage* over competitors. (By the way, *Unfair Advantage* does not mean doing anything illegal or unethical. See my definition of *Unfair Advantage* in the *Jim's Lexicon* section.) I call this the "Three Tiers of Marketing," and I first learned it a long time ago from Dan Kennedy. This system will revolutionize your thinking about marketing, and dramatically improve your results. I've coached a lot of floor dealers to use it to prioritize which marketing they do first.

Tier 1

This includes any marketing and sales efforts directed to your past customers, referrals, hot prospects, sphere of influence, etc.

These are the Tier 1 strategies you should begin with. Not coincidentally, these are the *Core 3* strategies we'll cover in Part 1.

- *Sales Closer System.* A carefully constructed sales process that leads prospects on a logical, step-by-step process from shopper to buyer. Gives <u>you</u> control of the sales process and creates total differentiation from competitors.

- *Referral Marketing System.* A sales and marketing process that farms your currently scheduled installations for immediate referral business.

- *"Herd Building"* Marketing System. Marketing to your <u>past</u> <u>customers</u> a minimum of once per month with fun, informative, valuable, entertaining communication that they look forward to receiving.

Tier 2

These are strategies for targeting people who don't know you, like you, trust you, or have any kind of relationship with you or your business yet. Here is a partial list:

- Website
- Direct mail
- Pay-per-click
- SEO
- Social media marketing
- Geographic-targeted marketing
- Demographic-targeted marketing
- Newspaper
- Valpak
- Display ads
- Trade shows/home shows
- Etc.

Tier 3

This is advertising done to a broad market, with very little targeting possible. There's a lot of waste. However, this doesn't mean it can't work. These media serve to supplement and reinforce the Tier 1 and Tier 2 strategies you have in place. To the largest degree possible, include Direct Response and lead generation mechanisms in this media, such as driving them to your website with an offer to get a free report or consumer's guide. This will give them the greatest chance of success, and help make them trackable.

- Radio
- Television
- Billboards

Implementing The Three Tiers

You should begin with Tier 1 (*Core 3*). Once your Tier 1 systems are up and running and generating money, then move on to Tier 2. But DO NOT do any Tier 2 until your Tier 1 is fully up and running and generating money. The only exception is your website, which you probably already have in place. Obviously you should keep it in place. However, don't invest time, energy, and money into SEO or other website/internet strategies until your Tier 1 is up and running. Once Tier 1 is in place, it makes sense to invest in developing a carefully engineered website/internet marketing strategy.

Once your Tier 2 strategies are up and running and generating money, then you may choose to move on to Tier 3. Use *luxury marketing* dollars for Tier 3.

During webinars and seminars I frequently teach the Three-Tier concept. I then ask the attendees where they spend the majority of their time, energy, and money. 95% or more say Tiers 2 and 3. The vast majority of floor dealers totally ignore Tier 1, preferring (out of ignorance) to jump straight to Tiers 2 and 3. Big mistake.

By using this system, you can make an intelligent, educated decision about which marketing to begin with. When an ad rep or web designer approaches you about buying their services, simply see which tier they fit into and decide whether or not you are ready to begin that advertising strategy.

Marketing Multipliers

Tier 1 strategies multiply the effectiveness of all your other marketing and advertising. Here's how:

Dwayne has a flooring dealership in a mid-size, Midwestern town. His average ticket for an installed residential floor is $3,000. He spends $5,000 on a direct mail campaign that generates 10 walk-ins. He has a 30% closed-sale batting average, so he closes three of them. This gives him gross sales of $9,000.

- $3,000 average ticket
- $5,000 spent on direct mail to generate 10 walk-ins
- 30% closed-sale batting average = 3 sales
- 3 sales x $3,000 average ticket = $9,000

Dwayne grossed $9,000 on this campaign. But let's say that he implements a *Sales Closer System,* so instead of closing 3 out of the 10, he closes 5. Let's also say that he implements a *Referral Marketing System,* so that out of the 5 closed sales he gets one referral. And let's say that he implements a past-customer marketing campaign so that over the next 12 months he gets an additional sale (either repeat business or a referral) from these six. Now he's up to 7 sales from the same $5,000 investment.

- 7 sales x $3,000 = $21,000

In this scenario Dwayne has generated 233% more revenue from the direct mail campaign. And this doesn't take into consideration that a good *Sales Closer System* has built-in upsell opportunities, so his average tickets will likely go up. It also doesn't take into consideration that repeat/referral customers generate higher margins. So in all likelihood, he will make significantly more money.

Now apply this to every other Tier 2 and Tier 3 campaign Dwayne is doing:

- Website
- SEO
- Direct mail
- Pay-per-click
- Display ads
- Radio
- TV
- Billboard
- Social media
- Valpak
- Etc.

By having the Tier 1 strategies in place, Dwayne exponentially multiplies the effectiveness of *all* his marketing efforts. This gives him an *Unfair Advantage* over every competitor in his market because all the others are still marketing by the seat of their pants.

In the next chapter we'll further explore the importance of Tier 1 strategies.

....

THREE

WHY THE *CORE 3* ARE NO LONGER OPTIONAL

FLOOR DEALER: It's getting harder and harder to close sales at full margin. It seems like people only care about who's the cheapest.

JIM: What strategies have you put in place to overcome this problem?

FLOOR DEALER: None. I don't know what to do.

The Tier 1 strategies are so critical to a dealer's success that within *Flooring Success Systems* we have developed an entire turnkey program dedicated to helping dealers get them implemented into their businesses quickly. This program is called *Core 3*, and includes:

1. **The *Design Audit*™.** This is our trademark-protected **_Sales Closer System_**. It's a carefully constructed sales process that leads prospects on a logical, step-by-step process from shopper to buyer, gives *you* control of the sales process, creates total differentiation from competitors, and other critical jobs.

2. ***Referral Connections*™.** This is our **_Referral Marketing System_** that farms your currently scheduled installations for immediate referral business.

3. **The *Neighborhood Advisor*™.** This is our **_Past Customer Marketing System_**, which includes a done-for-you monthly newsletter that you mail to your customers. It contains fun, informative, valuable, entertaining communication that they look forward to receiving. It also includes a weekly e-newsletter.

The *Core 3* includes training manuals, videos, and monthly training webinars that our members and their sales teams can attend for free. I say all this to emphasize how critical I believe the *Core 3* strategies to be for any dealer who wants to prosper and thrive in the 21st century. They are so vital to your success that we devote substantial resources to training dealers on these systems.

In upcoming chapters I will go into detail on the specifics of each of the *Core 3* strategies so you can implement them into your business, but first here are ...

9 Reasons Why The *Core 3* Strategies Are No Longer Optional If You Want To Succeed In The 21st Century

Throughout the remainder of this book, when I say *Core 3* I'm talking about the three strategies listed in Tier 1. I call them "Core" because they are foundational or central to any dealer's success, and because of the multiplier effect they have on all your other marketing and advertising efforts. When I talk about strategies from Tiers 2 and 3, I'll reference how they relate to the *Core 3*.

#1

The Marketing Multiplier effect

As you saw earlier, by having the *Core 3* in place you can increase your revenue from any Tier 2 or Tier 3 strategy by 200%-300% or more without significantly increasing your advertising costs.

#2

It's getting more and more expensive to acquire customers with Tier 2 and Tier 3 strategies

Once upon a time dealers could run a newspaper ad or direct mail campaign and count on those efforts to generate a consistent stream of business. Those days are long gone, likely never to return. In fact, I've polled hundreds of dealers during my webinars and live speaking events with this question: Is your advertising more effective, less effective, or the same as 10 years ago? 90% say less effective.

This doesn't mean you should never do display ads, radio, pay-per-click, social media, or other Tier 2 and Tier 3 strategies. Done correctly, these strategies can still work, and I coach dealers on *Direct Response Marketing* methods for being successful with them. Nevertheless, even when using my methods these strategies are still so expensive that you *must* have the Marketing Multiplier effect you get from *Core 3* in order to maximize your ROI. Therefore, before you invest time, energy, and money into Tiers 2 and 3, MAKE SURE you have your *Core 3* in place.

#3
Vanishing consumer trust

As I said earlier, consumers are growing ever more standoffish, skeptical, fearful, and mistrusting. They've been ripped off, disappointed, lied to, and scammed by corporations and their own government. They've been spied on by the NSA. They've been victimized by fraud, and/or they know someone who has. Our personal opinion on how bad these things are is irrelevant. It's what the great mass of consumers think and feel about them that matter, and they feel extremely vulnerable and distrusting. There are many ways the *Core 3* strategies overcome these problems, including that they position you and your sales team as Trusted Advisors, and they help you build, nurture, grow, and protect your "herd" of past customers so you can profit from them over and over again.

#4
Consumers are growing more distracted

Smartphones, social media, Facebook, television, Netflix, YouTube, and an ever-expanding toy box of distractions are all competing for your prospects' attention. It's very difficult and expensive (both in time and money) to cut through all the noise. If you go head-to-head with these distractions, prepare to sink more and more time, energy, and money into SEO, pay-per-click, Facebook, Pinterest, smartphone apps, and on and on.

However, the *Core 3* lets you play this game in a completely different way. This doesn't mean you should stop using SEO, Facebook, or other digital media. Instead, you do it with an emphasis on "herd" building, which is what *Core 3* is all about.

#5
Beat the boxes

Online retailers, discounters, and big boxes like Home Depot, Lowe's, Empire, and Lumber Liquidators can sink a fortune into "traditional" image advertising. They can blanket an entire market area a foot deep in snow drifts of promotional mailers. They can saturate the airwaves to create "name recognition." They can pour enormous amounts of time and money into bolstering their online presence. Simply put, they can outspend the vast majority of dealers.

However, their great weakness is that they are top-heavy, bureaucratic, red-tape-infested behemoths. This makes it impossible for them to create the personal connections with their customers (and their customers' sphere of influence) like you can with yours. People want to do business with people, not big, faceless, nameless, impersonal corporations. The *Core 3* creates those personal connections and gives you a huge advantage over the big boys.

You are also much more maneuverable than they are. The *Core 3* enables you to run circles around them like a speedboat running circles around the Titanic.

#6
The power of relationship marketing

Not long ago entire industries were built around telemarketing, and many businesses were totally dependent upon telemarketing to generate customers. A gigantic telemarketing industry emerged to service these businesses. With a stroke of a pen the government passed "do not call" laws, which, overnight, caused the collapse of many of these businesses. You now must have a consumer's permission before you call.

Anti-spam laws mean you must have permission to email consumers.

Same with fax.

Social media, SEO, and pay-per-click rules and regulations change constantly. A method that you are counting on to generate customers today can vanish tomorrow at the whim of Google, Facebook, or Twitter. It happens all the time.

Netflix, YouTube, and DVR have given consumers the power to watch *what* they want, when they want, with no commercials.

Streaming radio stations (Pandora) and satellite radio (Sirius) have given consumers the power to listen to commercial-free radio.

All of these factors are not only making advertising more difficult and expensive for dealers, they have reinforced consumers' resentment toward being interrupted by business "pitches," whether they arrive as an email, direct mail, a Facebook ad, or what have you.

The antidote to all of this is relationship marketing; developing a connection with your customers and their sphere of influence so they know you, like you, and trust you, and are eager to receive your communications and look forward to reading them. The *Core 3* strategies are totally focused on nurturing, growing, and protecting your herd of customers, and profiting from them. As Dan Kennedy says, they help transform you from "annoying pest" to "welcome guest."

Core 3 is also mostly immune to changes in laws, regulations, and rules, and for several reasons. First, a *Sales Closer System* happens in your dealership and in the customer's home. The same with a *Referral Marketing System*. And when a customer gives you their email and physical address they are giving you permission to contact them via those methods, so you can send them printed newsletters and e-newsletters. And since you have a relationship with them, and you are sending fun, informative, entertaining, welcome communication, they won't resent it. That is, they won't resent it as long as you're not sending them communication that's 100% pitch to buy something.

#7

Gain access to your customers' sphere of influence

Let's say you have a database with 1,000 past customers. Each one of those contacts has at least 200 people in their sphere of influence. By communicating consistently with them using fun, informative, entertaining material, and creating a "culture of referrals," you can tap into this larger sphere. Therefore, managed correctly, a "herd" of 1,000 customers gives you access to *at least* 200,000 people.

It's growing more expensive and difficult to reach those 200,000 people through traditional advertising methods. But the *Core 3* strategies essentially turn those 1,000 past customers into your personal ambassadors, selling your services to everyone they know.

#8

Miniscule marketing costs

A *Sales Closer System* and *Referral Marketing System* have no real marketing costs associated with them. Any additional sales generated by these methods cost you nothing in terms of marketing.

Marketing to your past customers via a monthly, printed, snail-mailed newsletter (supplemented with an e-newsletter) is dirt cheap in comparison to running ads on radio, TV, billboards, newspaper, Google, and elsewhere. And unlike all of these other methods, by mailing to your past customers you are laser-targeting the only people on the planet who are *proven* buyers of your products.

Let me say that again because it's so important I don't want you to miss it:

By mailing to your past customers you are laser-targeting the only people on the planet who are proven buyers of your products.

#9

Enormous profit potential in a short time

Here's a scenario I pose to floor dealers attending my webinars and seminars: *If you had in place a carefully engineered Sales Closer System that positioned you and your sales team as Trusted Advisors, created total differentiation from your competitors, and led consumers on a logical, step-by-step process transforming them from "shoppers" into "buyers," do you think closing an extra two sales per week per salesperson is reasonable?*

The vast majority say "yes."

So let's say you have three sales people and an average ticket of $3,000.

- $3,000 average ticket
- 3 sales people x 2 extra sales per week = 6
- 6 extra sales per week x $3,000 = $18,000 per week
- $18,000 x 52 weeks = $936,000 in extra revenue with NO MARKETING COSTS!

I work with dealers who have generated exponential growth far beyond the example above. However, if this sounds like a crazy, pie-in-the-sky number to you, cut it in half. The numbers are still amazing.

Here's another scenario I pose to dealers: *Let's say you have a carefully engineered referral marketing system that farms all your current installations for immediate referral business; do you think getting an extra two referrals per week per salesperson is reasonable?*

Again, the vast majority say "yes." Assuming the same average ticket and number of sales people as before, there's another $936,000 in extra sales with no marketing costs. And if this seems like a crazy, ridiculous number, cut in half. Either way, between these two strategies you are looking at extra sales of between $900k and $1.8 million without spending an extra dime on advertising.

But the fact is these numbers are actually conservative. All of the dealer success stories you're seeing in this book came about, in large part, because they've implemented the *Core 3*.

And we haven't even figured in the enormous profits you can generate by marketing to your past customers via a direct-response newsletter. This was the primary strategy used by Mark Bouquet from Illinois to take his business from near bankruptcy to being booked out for weeks in only six months. Every dealer I work with who is using a monthly direct-response newsletter is making money hand-over-fist with it, regardless of what part of the country or local economic conditions.

Here are just a few success stories from dealers who implemented the *Core 3*:

- Dan Ginnaty from Montana replaced all of his advertising with the *Neighborhood Advisor*™ newsletter strategy. His residential margins average 45%. He went from working 60-70 hours per week to working only 45. He takes weekends off and vacations every year.

- Garry Combs from Illinois went from near bankruptcy to opening his second store. He increased his residential margins to 50% across the board.

- Brent B. from Utah made an extra $250,000 his first year using the newsletter strategy.

- Craig Bendele from Florida increased his revenue by 50% in 12 months, then increased it by 50% again in the next 12 months. His residential margins are at 45%. He used to work 6-7 days per week, dark-to-dark. Now he arrives at 10:00 a.m., leaves at 5:00 p.m., and no longer works weekends.

- Jerome Nowowiejski from Texas went from residential margins of 15%-30% to 45%-50% in 90 days. He's also booked out 2-3 months. He now takes several 2-3 week vacations each year, and doesn't work weekends anymore.

There are many more examples of dealers who have used the *Core 3* to transform their businesses and their lives, but you get the point. Hopefully I've convinced you of the absolute necessity of having the *Core 3* implemented in your business.

....

FOUR

CORE 3 STRATEGY #1
SALES CLOSER SYSTEM

FLOOR DEALER: My sales people have a lousy closed-sale rate, and they always cave in and cut the price.

JIM: Do you have a step-by-step sales system, and have you trained them to use it?

FLOOR DEALER: No.

Back in the 1970's, McDonald's dramatically increased its revenue overnight by adding a simple sales system: *"Do you want fries with that?"* Upselling didn't cost them a single dime in advertising, but it has made them untold millions of dollars. It was basically "found" money. It was so successful that all the other fast food companies copied them.

Then they did it again in the 1980's with another sales system: packaged selling. McDonald's invented "Meal Deals," where the burgers came packaged up with fries and a drink. The upsells were built in. Again, millions in profits but not another dime spent in advertising. Once again Burger King, Taco Bell, and every other fast food seller under the sun copied them.

The point: Even small "tweaks" to your sales process can dramatically increase your revenue without increasing your costs. It's "found" money. An effective *Sales Closer System* will not only transform your closed sales, but it also provides these hard-to-identify, critical tweaks that can mean hundreds-of-thousands of dollars.

Does this story sound familiar …?

First, a customer walks into your store and spends an hour or more looking at samples. Then you have to drive out to her home, spend time chatting, and measure all the floors. Then you have to go back to your store, figure up the square footage, and get pricing from your distributor. Then you've got to put it all together into a bid and email it to her. You've got four hours—half a day—into this darn thing. *And it turns out that all the customer wanted was confirmation that she was getting a good deal from your competitor!* She jerked you around. How does it feel to be jerked around for half a day so the customer can feel better about going with one of your *competitors*?

If You Don't Have A System For <u>Selling</u>, You'll Always Be At The Mercy Of Your Customer's System For <u>Buying</u>

And their system for buying is to SHOP YOU. They'll come into your dealership, waste hours of your valuable time, and then buy from Home Depot. They'll use you for advice, and then turn around and buy online from Empire. How does it feel to have your time totally abused by customers?

If you want to beat the boxes and build a business that does $5 million/yr. with 45%-50% margins (or more), you've got to have a *Sales Closer System* in place so that *you* control the sales process.

Elements Of A *Sales Closer System*:

1. **Gives you total control of the process from the second a customer walks in your door.**

If you don't control the process, your customer *will*. And that means getting beat up on price, lost sales, and stomach ulcers.

2. **Quickly weeds out tire-kicking, price-shopping "bottom feeders.**

Some people are loyal to quality; some are loyal to price. About 10% of the population is totally loyal to cheapest price. They don't care about quality. They don't care about service. They are hardwired to buy from whoever is the cheapest. They are also hardwired to complain, cause problems, be suspicious, and give you migraines.

You *do not* want them as customers. (TIP: Once you identify a "bottom feeder," send them to your competitor! Let them have the headache.)

However, you often waste hours or days working up estimates before you figure out that you're dealing with a bottom feeder. They're "time vampires" who suck up hours of your time having you haul out samples, measure their home, and work up estimates. By the time you figure out that all they care about is cheap price, you have so much time invested that it's tempting to cave on price just to get the sale. Even then, you still may not get it because they'll take your "low" quote to your competitor and try to get them to beat it. These types are masters of playing you against your competitors.

And if you *do* get the sale? Heaven help you. They'll complain, moan, demand last-minute changes, and make your life hell.

This is why dealers I coach use a sales system that quickly identifies these types so they don't waste any time on them. A *Sales Closer System* identifies "bottom feeders" within a few minutes of their walking into your dealership so you can send them packing, and instead invest your valuable time on customers who appreciate you, who don't jerk you around, and who are happy to pay full margin.

3. **Positions you as a Trusted Advisor, like the family doctor.**

When a doctor makes a recommendation (like a prescription), their patients don't treat them with suspicion and haggle over price. They simply do what the doctor tells them to do. A *Sales Closer System* will position you like that family doctor so that customers simply take your recommendations. No suspicion, no haggling.

4. **Creates total differentiation from your competitors.**

If you don't create differentiation you wind up competing on price. The sales process is the "make it or break it" time to totally, utterly, and completely set yourself apart from competitors. A *Sales Closer System* does this automatically. Within 30 seconds of walking through your door, your customers are thinking, "This isn't like any of the other dealers I've visited." By the time you take them through the entire process they see you as absolutely different from the other dealers. Apples and oranges. They'll see everyone else as a bunch of dull, ordinary apples, and you as a bright, shiny, glowing orange.

5. **Automatically switches "shoppers" into "buyers."**

When a customer walks into your dealership, she is in "shopping" mode, not "buying" mode. The dealer who gets the sale is the one who's in front of her at that critical moment when she makes that switch to "buyer." If your sales process doesn't quickly move her from "shopper" to "buyer," she'll walk out your door and your competitor will steal the sale from you.

Average dealers "luck in" to sales because they happen to be in front of a customer when they make the "switch." It's not because they have a *Sales Closer System* in place. They just lucked out. (They also lose a lot of sales when the buyer makes the switch with one of their competitors.) Well, if you want to leave your competition in the dust you can't depend on luck. You should have a *Sales Closer System* in place that *makes* the switch happen while the customer is in *your* store.

6. **Increases your average ticket size.**

A question I ask dealers during training: How many flooring purchases happen as part of a larger remodeling or design project? Seldom or often? The majority say "often."

Then I ask: Do you have a sales system in place that *automatically* identifies the parts of a remodeling/design project where you can make additional profits, like counters, kitchen remodel, area rugs, window coverings, or other products? Then prompts your customer to purchase these as upsells? The majority say "no."

So we have the tragic situation where most flooring sales happen as part of a larger remodeling/design project, but most dealers don't have a system to capture these additional sales. *This is crazier than a rabid monkey!* You've already spent all the time, energy, and money to get the customer. By not having a *Sales Closer System* in place that identifies and captures these extra sales, you are leaving hundreds-of-thousands (possibly millions) of dollars on the table every year.

Dealers I coach know that they can add 25%-50% or more to most sales by securing those upsell opportunities. They see flooring as just the "boarding pass" to get into the customer's home so they can make upsells. They make sure their *Sales Closer System* reliably captures those extra sales on *every* job. With no high pressure! If you try to pressure people they will resent it. We all do. It's why everyone hates used car salesmen. Instead, a *Sales Closer System* makes upsell suggestions that don't *feel* like upsells to a customer. They feel like recommendations from a trusted professional, like a family doctor.

7. **Answers the unspoken question on every consumer's mind: Why should I do business with you instead of your competitor?**

If your sales system doesn't overwhelmingly, convincingly, and totally answer this question, you'll lose customers to any yahoo offering a cheaper price. A *Sales Closer System* does this automatically. It makes you the obvious choice, which leads to my next point ...

8. **Causes customers to independently arrive at the conclusion, "I'd have to be a complete idiot to buy from anyone else even if they're half the price."**

If you want to dominate your market and build a 5/45 business, it's not good enough that prospects "like" you, or "feel good" about you, or think you have great products. Not when 24/7 they hear your competitors screaming, "We'll give you the same thing cheaper!"

By the end of your sales process your customers must feel like they will be making the *biggest mistake of their life* if they buy flooring from *anyone else but you*, no matter how much cheaper they are. If you don't make this happen, you will lose tons of customers and hundreds-of-thousands of dollars to Home Depot or anyone else offering to sell on the cheap. A *Sales Closer System* does this for you automatically.

9. **It's brain-dead easy for a newbie salesperson to learn quickly, even if they have zero experience in the flooring business.**

If you are totally dependent on hiring sales people with flooring experience, you're causing big problems for yourself.

- What if there aren't any sales people with flooring experience immediately available?

- What if the only people with experience are total pains-in-the-you-know-what to work with? They know they've got you over a barrel, so they act like prima donnas. (This includes the pain-in-the-neck salesperson already on your team who thinks he's God's gift to flooring. You'd just LOVE to fire him. You fantasize about it. You dream about it. But you don't dare because you're worried about trying to find another salesperson with flooring experience.)

- What if you get the opportunity to hire a dynamite salesperson, but they don't have a background in flooring? You'll miss out on a very profitable opportunity.

The key is to have a *Sales Closer System* that can get total newbies selling like pros and making profits for your dealership within a couple of weeks. NEVER let yourself be held hostage by a jerk salesperson with an attitude just because they have experience in flooring.

10. **Enables you to command margins of 45%-50% or more.**

By having all these elements working together, you've created a sales powerhouse. You can write your own ticket. You can escape the cheap-price rat race of doom forever. You'll never sell on price again.

11. **Dramatically increases your sales *without* increasing advertising costs.**

Let's say you have a 30% closed-sale batting average. This means that if 10 people walk into your store, three wind up buying. If you increase that to six you've just *doubled your revenue* without increasing your costs by one thin dime. In fact, you'll save money because you're spending a lot less time with people who don't buy. A *Sales Closer System* (combined with the other *Zero-Resistance Selling Environment* strategies covered in this book) can get your closed sales to 80%-90% while at the same time keeping your prices up.

Why You Shouldn't Give A Rip About "Industry Averages."

I've had dealers say, *"Jim, when someone says they're closing 80% of their sales I don't believe them because the national average is 32%."* Let's get something straight ... I have no interest in teaching dealers how to be "average." I give dealers strategies that <u>blow the doors off "industry averages."</u> I want you to DOMINATE your market, beat the boxes, and make your competition eat your dust ... just like the dealers in this book are doing. If all you're interested in is being "average," you may as well stop reading now.

However, if you like the idea of gaining a massive <u>*Unfair Advantage*</u> over every competitor in your market, let's continue ...

Dealers Using My *Sales Closer System* Are Happy To Have Home Depot As A Neighbor

They know that Home Depot will lure "shoppers" into the area. Many of those shoppers visit their stores, and their *Sales Closer System* switches them to "buyer." **Home Depot actually generates sales for them!** Like they do for Mark ...

"We love having Home Depot as our neighbor! We take a lot of business from them!"
—Mark Bouquet, Illinois
(That's him in the photo)

Most of the dealers I work with are within a couple of miles of a Home Depot or other box store. Some are literally right across the street. They don't care. They love taking business from them, too!

Mike P., a dealer from Connecticut, increased his year-over-year revenue by 79% by introducing several new sales and marketing strategies into his business. Implementing a *Sales Closer System* was a big part of the mix.

The vast majority of flooring sales people have not been given a step-by-step sales process that walks prospects down a logical path from "shopper" to "buyer." They haven't been trained in a written process that can be learned, measured for results, and where they can be held accountable for results. As a result, most sales people wing it. This leaves far too much to chance, especially if you want to consistently command margins of 45%-50% or more.

Let's look at the four steps of a *Sales Closer System*.

Step 1:
Take Control Of The Sales Process

When a customer walks into a flooring store, most sales people make a critical mistake in the first 30 seconds that virtually guarantees they will get beat up on price and lose sales. Here's the mistake:

They say to the walk-in, *"How may I help you?"* or *"What kind of flooring do you have in mind?"*

Several bad things happen when a salesperson does this.

First, it creates no differentiation. If the prospect has visited other flooring stores, they've already heard this exact same opening line from their sales people. So you've created zero differentiation. You only have one chance to make a first impression, and an opener like this gives prospects the impression that you are exactly like everyone else.

Second, it gives the prospect control of the sales process. If you don't have a system for selling, you'll always be at the mercy of your prospect's system for buying. Therefore, it's critical that you take control of the sales process within the first 30 seconds of interaction with the prospect.

But when you ask, "How may I help you?" or "What kind of flooring did you have in mind?" this puts the prospect firmly in the driver's seat. The prospect replies, "I'm looking for laminate for my kitchen." The salesperson then schleps the prospect over to the laminate display. And what's the first question out of the prospect's mouth? "How much is this?" The prospect is now running the show. This also leads to the next problem.

Third, it introduces a premature price discussion. When a prospect asks about price, most of the time it's because they simply don't know enough about flooring to ask educated questions, so they ask the first thing that pops into their heads: *What's the price?* But the salesperson is already feeling stressed at having to deal with yet another "price shopper," and is mentally lowering the margins.

Price should never, ever, ever, ever come up until the end of the sales process, and at the exact time of your choosing. It should only happen after your prospect has gone through your entire *Sales Closer System* and has seen testimonials, guarantees, and warranties, been thoroughly wowed, and understands that you are utterly, totally, and completely different from all other dealers. Then when you present a price with 45%-50% margins they'll be much less price resistant. They'll understand why they should pay more. They'll "get it."

The Pattern Interrupt

So when a prospect comes into your store, instead of saying, "How may I help you?" or "What kind of flooring did you have in mind?" do something completely unexpected. I teach my dealers to say, "Welcome to Jimbo's Floors! Are you a new or returning customer? A new customer! Excellent! We have a special program for new customers. Can I take a quick minute and tell you about it?" If they are a returning customer say, "Excellent! We have a special program for returning customers. Can I take a quick minute and tell you about it?" Your "program" is your step-by-step *Sales Closer System*. Done correctly, 90%-95% of walk-ins will say "yes." This gives the salesperson instant control of the process and creates total differentiation.

This also acts as a pattern interrupt. The prospect walks into your store with her own agenda and expectations. She expects you to say the exact same thing she's heard at every other flooring store she's visited. Following this strategy interrupts this pattern, forces her to pause, and gives you the chance to take total control of the sales process.

Step 2:
Build Value

When a prospect agrees to hear about your "special program," you now have about 30 seconds to "sell" them on sitting down with you. For example, explain how there are thousands of flooring products, and your process will help narrow it down to the best product for their unique situation and lifestyle.

Step 3:
Ask Questions

When you visit your doctor, does he burst into the exam room and say, "Hey, we've got a 2-for-1 special on Viagra! Also, 50% off penicillin! And this week we're having our antidepressant blowout sale! Save up to 70% on Lexapro, Zoloft, and Prozac!"

No, those are used car salesman tactics. Instead he sits down with you, asks you questions, and writes down the answers in your chart. He finds out what's ailin' ya, and then (and only then) does he prescribe a course of treatment.

You want to position yourself as a Trusted Advisor, like the family doctor. Not like a used car salesman. An effective way to create the Trusted Advisor positioning is to ask lots of questions. So sit down with your prospect and ask questions about their lifestyle, level of traffic, the kind of flooring they currently own, how they've maintained it, etc. Write down the answers.

Target Questions

You want to ask questions that cause the prospect to paint a target on herself. This means the answers to these questions will hand you the keys to the sale. Here are some "target" questions to include:

- What's important about new flooring to *you*?
- What do you like about your current flooring?
- What do you dislike about your current flooring?
- Have you ever had flooring professionally installed?
- What did you like/dislike about the experience?
- What can we do to exceed your expectations?

Listen carefully to the answers to these questions because she will tell you what you need to know to get her to buy at margins of 45%-50% or more. It's almost a sure thing that no other dealer will have asked these questions, so by asking them you've created more differentiation.

If a prospect is unwilling to go through these first three steps, that's a good indication that they are a price shopper, and that you may not want to invest a lot of time with them. Proceed with caution.

Step 4:
The In-Home Visit

Most dealers simply show up, take measurements, leave, and then email or call the prospect with a price. This is an enormous missed opportunity to wow the prospect, create differentiation, and position yourself as a Trusted Advisor.

When the salesperson visits a prospect's home to measure, he should be trained to not only get measurements, but also to inspect her vacuum, the walk-off mats, the kind of carpet spotter she is using, etc. He should also give written recommendations on floor maintenance.

Your entire process should be written out, including sales scripts for each stage of the process.

Finally, a word of warning: This kind of system has been proven to work in my own businesses, and by the many dealers I've trained to do it. But occasionally a dealer will tell me that many of their walk-ins won't go through the process. Invariably, upon further questioning, I find out that the dealer is not using sales scripts, or in some other way is messing up the process. So if you get pushback from a high percentage of walk-ins, don't assume they are all price shoppers. And don't give up on this system: It works. Look at what you and your team may be doing to inadvertently sabotage your results.

How A New-To-The-Industry Sales Person Increased His Closed Sale Ratio To 85% With High Margins

A big challenge for dealers is finding sales people with experience in the flooring industry. If none are to be found, dealers must hire people without experience, which means many months of training before they become producers for the business. And after all that work? Often the salesperson will quit, or go to work for a competitor. But what if there's a better way? What if you could get a total newbie salesperson producing big revenue for your business in just weeks instead of months?

That's exactly what happens for dealers who use a *Sales Closer System* I developed called the *Design Audit™*. Daniel Knigge (photo, right) is a salesperson for Russ Bundy (left), a dealer from Utah. Daniel had very little experience in the flooring business when he began using the *Design Audit*. Here's what Daniel told me:

"I started only six months ago in the flooring business. I'm very green. Before using the *Design Audit* my residential margins were 30%-35%. It was emotionally stressful. I'd end the day, be totally exhausted, and realize I hadn't closed any sales. It was discouraging. We're right down the street from two home stores. People would come in and say, 'Lowe's quoted me this price,' or 'Home Depot quoted me such and such.' I was constantly having to compete on price. I started using the *Design Audit* just a couple of months ago. I closed the first seven out of seven people that I used the *Design Audit* on. Since then my overall close ratio has averaged 85%. Our residential margins are now averaging 40%."

I asked Russ how it feels having a system that you can turn over to a totally new, green, never-worked-in-the-flooring-business-before salesperson, and have him instantly begin generating these kinds of margins and close ratios. Here's what he said:

"It's pretty amazing, and gives me a lot of hope about building my business. In the past I felt like it's really hard to bring someone new in. It takes a couple of years to get them trained. What if during that time they aren't successful, and they don't generate enough money, and you have to start over from scratch? So to be able to put somebody into a system takes a lot of pressure off of me from needing to teach them everything about how to close a sale. The tools are there for them to be able to do that with the *Design Audit*. Hiring a new salesperson is always kind of scary; it's kind of a crapshoot. I think other dealers can relate to this. You can bring in a good person, but put them into a bad sales system, and they may not last very long. But you can bring a mediocre person in and put them in the right system, and even they can be successful. We're also getting higher margins by using the *Design Audit*. **So even though we cut all our advertising, our net profits have literally tripled.**"

....

FIVE

CORE 3 STRATEGY #2
REFERRAL MARKETING SYSTEM

JIM: What percentage of your business comes from referrals?

FLOOR DEALER: About 40%.

JIM: Since that's the single biggest source of new customers for you, do you have a marketing system in place to maximize referrals?

FLOOR DEALER: Uh ... no.

5 Reasons Why Referrals Are The Best Form Of Marketing To Get New Customers

1. Customers who are referred to you are already "pre-sold" on your service. Whoever referred them has already sold them on the idea that you're the best. They are much, much easier to sell to than a suspicious, standoffish, tire-kicking prospect brought in by "traditional" advertising.

2. You get the "halo" effect. Other people saying how great you are always sounds better than *you* saying how great you are. When other people brag about you and refer their friends, they are giving you a halo. They are making you look good without you saying a word.

3. Skepticism is very low. After all, if their brother-in-law, or aunt, or best friend bought from you, you must be pretty darned fantastic!

4. Referrals have very low price resistance. It's much, much easier to command margins of 45%-50% (or more) than with "bottom feeders" brought in by "traditional" advertising.

5. Referrals have *zero* marketing costs. You avoid the massive advertising costs required to get a price-resistant, skeptical "stranger" who doesn't trust you in the door.

This is extremely powerful, but most dealers miss the importance of referrals. Think about it. With a referral, you are being handed a pre-sold, non-skeptical customer with low price resistance who sees you with a "halo" ... and it costs you nothing!

In spite of this, only a tiny fraction of dealers have a *Referral Marketing System* in place to dramatically increase their referrals. (Of those that do, many of them are in my club.) For most dealers, referrals are a "happy accident." They do a decent job, and eventually they get some referrals. But there is no *Referral Marketing System* in place to cause a referral "explosion."

Having A *Referral Marketing System* Is No Longer A Luxury

Most "traditional" advertising doesn't work very well, except to lure in price-shopping, skeptical, stand-offish consumers. As traditional advertising continues to lose its effectiveness, having a dependable method to dramatically increase referrals is a necessity if you want to prosper. This means having a *Referral Marketing System* in place.

Given how critical referrals are to your success, does it make sense to depend on a "happy accident" to get referrals? Not if you want to beat the boxes and build a $5 million flooring business with 45%-50% margins.

An Effective *Referral Marketing System* Will Do These 9 Jobs:

1. Dramatically increase your sales each month.

2. Generate an average of (at least) three instant referrals from every sale. Of those three, one will need flooring right away.

3. Create good obligation. Customers feel obligated to give you referrals, in the same way they feel obligated to pay you.

4. Generate ongoing referrals from customers throughout the seven years between sales.

5. Create the "bandwagon" effect. Customers who refer are given "celebrity status," thus prompting other customers to refer because they want to be celebrities, too.

6. Enable sales people who are "newbies" to the flooring industry to have instant success getting referrals.

7. Activate your customer's "Referral Radar," so any time the subject of flooring comes up with their friends, relatives, neighbors, and coworkers, they refer you on the spot without even having to think about it.

8. Convince your customers that they are doing the socially responsible thing by referring you. That they are doing their friends and relatives a huge favor whenever they refer you.

9. Turn your entire list of past customers into an army of sales people for your business.

Why Referral "Postcards" Are A Joke

Referral postcards you send to customers (or leave at their house) and hope they'll fill out and mail back are mostly a big waste of time and effort. They won't do any of the nine things I just mentioned.

Maybe you've used referral postcards or something similar. If so, how many of them have you actually gotten back? Probably not very many. This tactic doesn't work for the 9,000 other dealers using it either. Yeah, you may get a few of those cards back, but you will never create the flood of referrals that a *Referral Marketing System* doing those nine jobs can generate.

Some dealers reward their customers for referring. This isn't a bad idea; it's just incomplete. Unless you combine that with the "Celebrity Status," "Referral Radar," "Good Obligation," and other elements I mentioned, it has very limited effectiveness. By and large, people don't refer because you reward them. You've got to have those other elements in place.

Why Referrals Are Critical To Your Success

It's pop-quiz time! Check all the statements that apply to your business.

- ❑ Is advertising less effective than it used to be?

- ❑ When advertising *does* work, does it tend to attract price shoppers?

- ❑ Are prospects more distrusting than they used to be?

- ❑ Are consumers more price sensitive than ever before?

- ❑ Are prospects more standoffish than ever before?

- ❑ Do prospects "shop around" much more than they used to?

- ❑ Do consumers take longer to make a purchase decision than they used to?

If you checked any of these you are not alone. These are challenges that plague most dealers. They also highlight why relationship marketing is ceasing to be a luxury and quickly becoming a necessity if you want to survive and prosper in flooring retail. This is why referral marketing is so vital to your success.

Most Dealers Don't Have An "On-Purpose" Referral Marketing System In Place

What The...?!

Imagine the owner of a multimillion-dollar home. They want hardwood installed throughout. This is easily a $50,000+ job. Where do you think they are going to look for a flooring dealer? In the newspaper? Online? On the radio?

Fat chance.

They are going to ask people in their sphere—other million-dollar home-owners—who they bought their floors from.

The dealers I coach routinely get their largest sales from referrals. Here are just a few examples:

Mark from Illinois landed a multi-state, high-six-figure commercial account from a referral.

Dan from Montana got his first $100,000 commercial account from a referral. He got a 50% margin on this sale, virtually unheard of for a commercial job, especially one this size.

Brent from Utah got a $40,000 residential job from a referral from a Realtor.

Jimmy from North Carolina regularly sells $10,000, $20,000, $30,000+ residential jobs, and virtually all of them come from referrals.

Jerome from Texas routinely does residential sales in excess of $10,000, most from referrals.

Think back to *your* 10 largest sales of the past year. I'll bet you the biggest pizza in Chicago that seven or eight of them came from repeat/referral customers.

5-Step *Referral Marketing System*

Referrals are so valuable that you should not passively wait for your customers to send you referrals. But that's exactly what most floor dealers do. At best, referrals are a "happy accident." By having a *Referral Marketing System* in place you can dramatically increase the number of referrals you get.

Here are the steps to the *Referral Marketing System* that I teach floor dealers:

Step 1:
Be Referable

Being referable is the first and most critical step to getting referrals. I know it sounds obvious, but a lot of dealers neglect this, so it needs to be said. You've got to provide great service and great products if you want referrals.

Great service begins with the basics, what I call "blocking and tackling."

- Return phone calls promptly.
- Show up on time.
- Call your customer five minutes before you arrive at their home.
- Dress professionally.
- Say "please" and "thank you."
- Be courteous and polite.
- Honor your warranties and guarantees.
- Under promise, over deliver.
- Be honest, especially if you have to give your customer bad news, like their special order of hardwood got delayed because of a blizzard.
- Do what you say you're going to do, when you say you're going to do it.

If you're unwilling to do these basic things, you'll always struggle to get referrals. Don't ignore the basics.

Step 2:
Schedule A Follow-Up Visit

Meet with your customer after the installation is complete. I recommend doing this in their home, but if that's not possible you can also do it in your store. Use the following script:

"Mrs. Jones, now it's time to schedule your post-installation follow-up visit. John will do a walkthrough with you and inspect the installation to make sure everything is perfect. Are mornings or afternoons better for you?"

Notice that I don't say, "Can we meet?" That gives her a yes or no option. Instead I give her two yes options: morning or afternoon. I also treat the follow-up visit as standard and customary; part of the usual process, just like scheduling the installation.

If you can't get to the customer's home, schedule an appointment for her to come into your store to meet with the salesperson. Tell her that you've got a thank you gift for her.

Step 3:
Wow The Customer

- Arrive on time. Call a few minutes before you arrive for your appointment.
- Bring a surprise gift for the customer.
- Wear medical shoe covers.
- Once inside, do a walkthrough and make sure the installation looks good. Oooh and aaah over the flooring, reinforcing to the customer what a great choice she made.

Step 4:
Referral Request

Most dealers never ask for referrals. At best they use an "oh, by the way approach" and say something like, "I'm glad you are happy with your new floors, Mrs. Gopherhoser. We'd really appreciate it if you passed our name along to anyone you know who needs flooring." This is not going to generate many referrals beyond what you are already getting.

The dealers I coach use an "on-purpose" referral request strategy. First, they transition from inspecting the floors to educating their customer on their referral program. This transition is carefully scripted: "Mrs. Smith, now I'd like to take a minute and tell you about our referral program."

Next, they use an actual referral form. Some points to include when designing your own form should include:

- **Let her know that advertising is very expensive, so rather than pay the TV or radio station, you'd rather reward your customers.**

- **She'll be doing her friends a HUGE favor by referring a company they can trust.**

- **Each of her referrals will get a gift certificate to your store in her name.**

This form actually sells her on all the benefits of your referral program to her and her friends. The form should also include spaces for the names of people she wants to refer.

If you can't possibly meet with her in her home, then let her know you've got a thank you gift waiting at your store, and schedule an appointment for her to meet with her salesperson. Present her with your referral program and referral form while she's in your store.

> ## Watch Out! ⚠ Don't Expect Customers To Mail In Referral Forms
>
> Leaving a referral form or card behind and hoping the customer will mail it in doesn't work very well. You'll be waiting for the next ice age. In order for this strategy to be fully effective you should meet with your customer in person.

Step 5:
Referral Follow-Up

Not every person who is referred to you will need flooring right that minute, but that doesn't mean those contacts aren't valuable. If you market to them correctly, many will convert into sales when they are ready to purchase flooring. Here's what I recommend doing:

You just installed floors for Suzie Smith and she's thrilled, so she fills out your referral form and gives you five names. Send each referral a letter with a gift certificate to your store.

Let's say you get 50 referrals in a month by doing this. Will all of them need flooring right this minute? Of course not, but 5 to 10 of them will. If your average ticket is $3,000, then that's an extra $360,000 in sales per year. Subscribe the ones who didn't purchase right away to your monthly newsletter. Many of them will convert into sales over the next 1 to 2 years.

The people who don't purchase immediately are incredibly valuable leads. Think about it: They've been referred to your business by someone they know. They got a letter from you introducing yourself. Enclosed in the letter is a gift certificate from their friend. Then each month they get your fun, entertaining, informative, educational newsletter. Who do you think is going to be at the top of the list when they are finally ready to purchase floors? What do you think the results will be when you send a special offer to this list compared to a list you purchased? Night and day difference. Many times I and the dealers I coach have had referrals—who haven't even purchased yet—send us referrals because they are so impressed with the follow-up.

How Each Of Your Sales People Can Generate An EXTRA $312,000

Most dealers would agree that if they trained their sales team to use a *Referral Marketing System* that each salesperson could close an extra two sales per week. The revenue adds up very quickly:

Average ticket: $3,000

2 extra sales per week = $6,000

$6,000 x 52 weeks = $312,000

That's $312,000 per year in extra revenue *per salesperson* with no marketing costs! If this seems like a crazy, unrealistic, pie-in-the-sky number, cut it in half. You're still at $156,000 in extra revenue per salesperson. If you have three sales people you've just added $468,000 to $936,000 per year without increasing your marketing budget by one penny!

CASE STUDY

How David Made An Extra $90,463 In One Month

Having a *Referral Marketing System* in place can produce big revenue gains in a short time, like it did for David Kocian.

David owns Guarantee Carpet, Inc., in Corpus Christi, Texas, and has been in business since 1984. When I first met David in 2008, he had been advertising his business the same way most dealers do: print ads, website, television, etc. The previous year he had spent $60,000 in print ads and $35,000 in television ads. "The ads didn't even pay for themselves," he told me. "It's so frustrating to invest money on the advice of an advertising rep, and then get little to no response." Many dealers can relate.

He was desperate to find a way to market his store that worked; to stop throwing away money on ads that did nothing but suck his bank account dry. "I was totally fed up with spending money on ads, willy-nilly, with no true marketing plan or system that would produce consistent results," he told me.

After he joined *Flooring Success Systems* he began to implement the *Core 3* strategies, including the Referral Connections™ system. The results were amazing. "I made an extra $90,463 in one month! During a slow economy!" he told me. Remember, this was 2008 and the "Great Recession" was in full swing.

"My sales people had huge grins on their faces as they turned in their paperwork each week," he went on to tell me. "They were thrilled at how much revenue we were generating with just one simple strategy. It's hard to describe how good that felt!"

Roughly half of the $90k came from a single job, which isn't surprising. Think back to your last 10 large jobs; chances are that most of them were repeat or referral customers. This is because when people are going to buy tens-of-thousands of dollars in flooring they usually get referrals. There's too much money at stake to risk hiring someone off a website or a radio ad.

By having a *Referral Marketing System* in place you will not only increase the number of average-sized sales, but you'll put yourself in a position to land more of the larger jobs that usually can't be had through traditional advertising.

....

SIX

CORE 3 STRATEGY #3 THE DIRECT RESPONSE CUSTOMER NEWSLETTER

JIM: How many customers do you have in your database?

FLOOR DEALER: About 5,000.

JIM: So you have 5,000 proven buyers of your products. How often do you market to them?

FLOOR DEALER: Never.

New customers who come to you through "traditional" advertising have a ton of baggage. They are skeptical, mistrustful, price sensitive, harder to close, they complain more, and on and on. Not so with your past customers. They already know you, like you, and trust you. They are far easier to sell to.

Benefits of working with past customers (check any that sound familiar)

❑ You avoid the massive advertising costs that it takes to get a new customer to walk through your door. This savings goes right back in your pocket. It's basically "found money."

❑ Past customers are pre-sold. On a "ready to buy" scale of 1-10, past customers are 9's and 10's. (New customers from "traditional" advertising are mostly 1's and 2's, and you have to do all the hard work of moving them up to 10 before they will buy. Oftentimes you'll lose them to a cheap-price competitor long before that.)

❑ They are much more willing to pay premium prices than strangers.

❑ They are much more pleasant to work with because there's already a relationship. They don't treat you like a criminal out to rip them off.

❑ They are much easier to sell to ... in fact, they don't require much "selling." They already know they are going to buy from you. They just want your help in selecting their flooring.

❑ Past customers refer their friends, relatives, neighbors, and coworkers.

In spite of all these benefits, the vast majority of dealers totally ignore their past customers. Instead, they spend all their time, energy, and money using "traditional" advertising to try to get distrustful strangers to buy from them. Does this make sense? Not if you want a $5 million business with 45%-50% margins.

That's Why It's Critical To Have A "Herd Building" Marketing System In Place

Your biggest profits come from past customers. You're leaving a fortune on the table if you neglect to put a marketing system in place to fence in your herd, nurture your herd, and protect your herd from poachers. By making this one critical shift in your thinking—from being a "floor dealer" to being a "Rancher"—you will totally transform your business and your life. You'll leave your competitors in the dust, including Home Depot. Why? Because the vast majority of dealers will never make that shift.

WARNING: If you are unwilling to make that shift, and another dealer in your area **is** willing, then you'll probably wind up eating *their* dust. Through *Flooring Success System's* educational efforts, more and more dealers are shifting to the "Rancher" concept, so be careful you're not the last one to the party.

An Effective Herd Building System Will Do The Following:

- Position your business as the obvious choice.

- Create total differentiation from your competitors. As discussed earlier, if you don't create differentiation you will wind up competing on price.

- Create total Top of Mind Awareness by keeping your business name in front of past customers week in and week out. You don't know when a customer will be ready to buy, so you must stay constantly in front of them with fun, informative, entertaining, valuable, welcome information so when

83

the time comes you're the *only* dealer they even think about working with.

- Get your customers into your store *before* they go shopping online. Your past customers should not have to search online to find you. Lots of dealers think, "Well, my customers can Google flooring and find me." BAD IDEA! Sending your past customers online to find you is like sending a sheep into a pack of wolves! All your competitors are lurking there ready to gobble them up with "cheap-price" offers!

- Enable you to escape the cheap-price rat race of doom forever, and allow you to command premium prices (45%-50% margins, or better).

- Fence your past customers *in* and keep poachers *out*.

- Increase the frequency that customers buy from you. (Yes, you *can* increase how often they buy flooring from you.)

- Dramatically increase your referrals.

- Position you and your sales team as Trusted Advisors rather than "used car salesmen."

- Create a sense of "Community" among your past customers.

- It's much more affordable than many other forms of advertising

- It builds lasting, undying loyalty.

"Jeez, Jim. Is There A Strategy That Will Do All That?"

Yes, but only a tiny handful of dealers know about it or do it. (Of those that do, many of them are in my club. It's another reason I decided to write this book: to get the word out.) The strategy is a monthly printed *Direct Response Newsletter*, supplemented with a weekly *Direct Response e-newsletter*. This means you are getting in front of your past customers—*proven* buyers—64 times per year. (By the way, don't worry if you don't have your customers' email addresses. Many of the dealers you're meeting in this book didn't either. They began with a printed newsletter, and then added the e-newsletter later, as they gathered email addresses.)

Some dealers think that this much communication will turn off past customers and annoy them. Maybe you even think that. Well, that leads me to my next point ...

Why Most "Past Customer" Advertising Reeks Like Expired Cheese

If you send 64 messages per year that are 100% about flooring to your past customers, heck yeah you're going to annoy them! I know of dealers who e-blast their list with one "special" after another. People hate that stuff. Do you like getting an email box full of spammy sales offers? Well, neither do your customers.

So I'm not talking about doing *anything* like that.

I'm also not talking about sending out a boring newsletter, like your insurance company sends you. You know, it's 100% about insurance. BORING. I call them "snooze-letters."

Instead, you should use a monthly *Direct Response Newsletter*, supplemented with a weekly *Direct Response e-newsletter*. It should contain fun, informative, entertaining, valuable, welcome content. It should be so much fun that your customers look forward to getting it, eagerly open it up the minute it arrives, and are thoroughly entertained when reading it. It should be so interesting that they share it with their friends, and forward the e-newsletters to them. A good *Direct Response Newsletter* should also include emotional triggers that compel your customers to buy from you and send referrals to you.

A good *Direct Response Newsletter* is the foundation of an effective herd building marketing system. In fact...

It's How Mark Turned Around His Failing Business

A monthly *Direct-Response Newsletter* was the primary strategy he used to go from nearly closing his doors to being booked out for weeks ... *in only six months.* Not long after that he did over $3 million.

Dealers all over the U.S. and Canada are using this strategy to rake in tremendous profits, cement customer loyalty, and totally eliminate the "feast-or-famine" cycle.

Customers Demand That The Newsletter Be Forwarded To Them When They Move

Think back to the last time you moved. Did you contact all the companies sending you junk mail and give them your forwarding address so they could keep sending you junk? Of course not. In fact, you probably sort your mail over a trash can and toss out *unopened* anything that even looks like junk mail. Your customers do the same thing with their junk mail, including the slick, glossy advertisements *you* spend thousands of dollars mailing to them.

Well, check this out ... dealers in my club use a done-for-them Direct Response newsletter that I provide them called the *Neighborhood Advisor*™. My dealers regularly get calls from customers who have moved to give them their forwarding address so they can keep getting the newsletter!

I've been using *Direct Response Newsletters* for almost 20 years, and I've had the same thing happen many times. There is simply *no other advertising* that will do this. It doesn't exist. Period. My dealers get stopped in grocery stores by customers telling them how much they enjoy the newsletter. Customers walk into their stores holding the newsletter. Talk about "herd building!" Again, *no other advertising* can do this.

IMPORTANT! All flooring is all boring. Your newsletter should be 90% fun, valuable, entertaining content, and only 10% about flooring. Otherwise it will be like those boring insurance "snooze-letters." You will not get responses like my dealers and I get.

How To Use Customer Distrust And Skepticism To Create Undying Loyalty

As discussed earlier, the buying public has been lied to and ripped off by floor dealers, politicians, Wall Street, internet scammers, etc. This is a business-destroying problem for most dealers, but you can turn it into an advantage. Here's how:

All this fear and skepticism has made consumers terrified of buying high-ticket items (like flooring) from strangers. They are scared to death of losing thousands or tens-of-thousands of dollars to a flooring company that rips them off. This is why new customers brought in by "traditional" advertising are so standoffish and skeptical.

SO ... if you're the dealer in your town who has a "Herd Building" marketing system in place, who do you think is going to get the business? *You* are, of course! In fact, by using a *Direct Response Newsletter,* you are constantly reminding them that, "Hey! You DO know a flooring company you can trust, and who you can send referrals to." This is a massive relief to your customers. They don't have to worry about getting ripped off, or lied to, or throwing away thousands of dollars because an incompetent dealer sold them the wrong flooring.

Your customers are willing to pay *more* for this security. Let me say that again because it's important: ***Your customers are willing to pay more for this security.*** This translates into dramatically increased sales, a huge jump in referrals, and being able to command margins of 45%-50% or more.

Many Of Your Customers Forget About You Between Purchases

The national average for flooring replacement is about seven years. That is a long, *long* time between purchases. Plenty of time for poachers to sneak in and steal many members of your herd.

Do you think that just because you did a good job for a customer that they are going to automatically think of you seven years later when they are finally ready to buy flooring again? After seven years of seeing literally *thousands* of commercials promoting Home Depot, Lowe's, and Empire? After seven years of seeing *thousands* of "cheap-price" advertisements from your competitors?

Dream on.

When they're ready to buy flooring, they're going to think of *whoever is in front of them that week*. Will that be you ... or your competitors?

The only way to counter this onslaught is to stay in front of your customers week in and week out with fun, informative, valuable, entertaining, welcome communication they look forward to getting, and will actually read. And *guarantees* that when the time comes for them to buy flooring (or refer someone) that it's YOU—the one they know, like, and trust—in front of them. And the only affordable, effective tool that *guarantees* this will happen is a monthly *Direct Response Newsletter* and a weekly *Direct Response e-newsletter*.

14.3% Of Your Customers Will Replace Their Flooring This Year

If the average replacement time for flooring is every seven years, then each year 14.3% of your database will replace their flooring. A newsletter sent to your entire database will help ensure that 14.3% will come back to you rather than some hack offering to sell to them on the cheap.

How To Create Your Own Newsletter

Here are some guidelines on assembling an effective newsletter:

Use infotainment, meaning make your newsletter content a mix of 90% entertainment (fun, general-interest articles that have nothing to do with floor covering) and 10% information about your business. This is because in any given month most of your past customers don't need floor covering right then, so don't bore them with 100% floor covering content. That would be like getting a newsletter from your dentist each month and the entire thing was about the latest advances in root canal surgery. Boring.

Another important component is to include emotional triggers that compel readership, and get customers to buy from you and refer people in their sphere of influence to you. Here are some of the most important triggers:

- Photo of you on the first page. This puts a human face on your company. People want to do business with people, not impersonal corporations. You can also include photos of your staff.

- "Did You Know" section. This gives the reader some info on your flooring business that they may not know. For example, that you sell window coverings.

- Contest. This can be a trivia contest, referral contest, etc.

- Testimonials. You should include testimonials in all your marketing materials.

- Acknowledge new customers, returning customers, and those who referred.

- Promote your referral program.

One floor dealer I was coaching left out many of the triggers listed above, and the newsletter got little to no response. I caught the mistake and immediately coached him on what to do. He put the triggers back in and response shot up.

Send your printed newsletter monthly. Some dealers I know have switched to sending it every other month and have seen their sales drop during the "off" months. They quickly switched back to sending it monthly.

Don't make your newsletter slick and glossy, or use four-color printing. Black printing on white or colored paper is the way to go. This makes it look very personal, like you hammered it out on your computer and sent it out. This has the added advantage of being much less expensive to print.

I've found that the best newsletter length is four pages, with an optional insert. You don't have to make it 20 pages long. I have them printed on a single sheet of white or colored 11x17 paper. This folds up nicely to fit in a standard business envelope.

Have patience. A monthly newsletter is a relationship-building tool as well as a marketing strategy. It can take a little time to reestablish a connection with past customers, especially if they haven't heard from you in a while. Some dealers luck out and get instant response the first time they send one out; others take a few months of consistent monthly mailings before they begin to see results. However, every single dealer I work with who is sending out a monthly newsletter is making money from it. Done correctly, a monthly direct-response newsletter will work. Period.

Weekly E-Newsletter

I've had dealers ask me, "Can't I just email my newsletter?" You can, but your results will suffer. Emails have lower implied value than printed letters; it's too easy to hit the "delete" button. A four-page newsletter, like the one described above, doesn't make a good email because it's too long. Yes, you can send it as a PDF attachment, but these don't get good open rates. I've been using and teaching newsletter strategies since 1997, and I can tell you that emailed newsletters don't work nearly as well as printed ones. However, an e-newsletter can be a great *supplement* to your printed letter. The best way to do an e-newsletter is to stick with the 90/10 rule: 90% fun, informative, value-added, entertaining information and about 10% about flooring. Your e-newsletter should contain a short, general-interest article that's fun to read (100-200 words). At the end include a short blurb about your business with a link to your website and a phone number. You should also include a testimonial.

Have realistic expectations. Even a well done e-newsletter may get only a 20% open-rate, which is far lower than a newsletter sent via snail mail, but it doesn't cost you anything to send. And as long as you are providing fun, informative information (and not boring them with 100% flooring advertising), most people won't opt out and you'll be able to stay in front of them week after week.

CASE STUDY

Dan Quit All "Traditional" Advertising Cold Turkey, His Margins Are At 45% Or More, And His Store Is Thriving!

Dan Ginnaty's flooring dealership is in Great Falls, Montana. Like many dealers he got an early start in flooring. His dad was an installer, so he's been around the business since he was 5 years old.

Dan cancelled almost all of his traditional advertising (going "cold turkey," as he put it) and replaced it with a direct-response newsletter I provide dealers called the *Neighborhood Advisor*™. It has all the elements and emotional triggers described above. The newsletter has become his major tool for marketing to previous customers and new prospects. Since switching from Tier 3 advertising to the newsletter his response is quantifiably superior.

His customers call when they move to provide their new address so they can receive his newsletter at their new home. I asked Dan if he ever got this response from customers with traditional advertising. "Never happened," he said.

Which makes sense. Think back to the last time you moved. Did you call all the companies sending you advertisements and give them your forwarding address? Of course not. But dealers sending a direct-response newsletter get those calls regularly. This is because this type of newsletter is more like getting a magazine than an advertisement.

Not only is Dan getting customers through the newsletter, but the type of customer is different. "We're talking to people on a monthly basis minimum who have proven that they will give us their money in the past, and the likelihood that they'll do so in the future is greatly improved over someone listening to the radio or seeing you on TV." Dan has seen that the way they are perceived and received by the consumer is different: "They're almost friends when they come in. They know what we look like because we have our picture in the newsletter ... it's very friendly."

And unlike most "traditional" flooring ads, Dan's newsletter doesn't rely on "cheap-price" offers to get people in the door. "My residential margins are at 45%," Dan told me recently. "And I just did a $120,000 commercial job with 50% margins."

Complimentary 1-Hour Dealership Diagnostic

I'll personally give you a diagnostic of your market area to help you overcome the **"7 Deadly Problems,"** and to see if your business is a good candidate to **generate $5 Million/year with 45% margins or better**. Here's what we'll do during our hour together:

First, I'll ask you some questions about your business to help me understand **where you are at right now**, including:

- The population of your market area
- How many hours per week you're working vs. how many you'd like to work
- Advertising you're currently doing
- How much you're making vs. how much you'd like to make
- Who your biggest competitors are, etc.

Next we'll discuss where you **would like to be**.

- Increasing your income
- Eliminating the "feast or famine" cycles in your business
- Working less than 40 hours per week, no weekends, lots of vacations, etc.
- Having a stress-free business

Then I'll give you my best solutions for bridging the gap between **where you are and where you want to be**. I've done hundreds of Dealership Diagnostics, and most dealers have an "a-ha moment" when they see the solution to their problem right in front of them. You'll leave our meeting together with a game plan to overcome your problems and reach your goals! How awesome will THAT feel!

How To Secure Your Dealership Diagnostic...
Call us at 1-877-887-5791

A member of my team will schedule your appointment with me on the spot.

My normal fee for a Dealership Diagnostic is $500, but because you got my book I'll give it to you on a complimentary basis for a limited time.

Sales & Marketing Training For Your Organization

Are you a distributor, manufacturer, vendor, trade organization, trade show, or other organization serving the flooring industry? Jim can provide sales and marketing training for your group of flooring retailers, either in person or via webinar.

During Jim's trainings dealers learn how to **create total differentiation from their competitors, charge premium prices, and explode their profits in any market.** They also learn how to make their dealerships system-dependent rather than owner-dependent, thus enabling them to achieve higher levels of success, while at the same time having a fulfilling life outside their business.

The biggest strength about Jim's teaching method is that it's not textbook theory. Instead he gives dealers strategies he has been developing and using in his own businesses since 1993. They have been tested, tweaked, adjusted, and proven in hundreds real world flooring businesses from across the U.S. and Canada. Dealers walk away from Jim's sessions with actionable, nuts-and-bolts strategies they can use immediately to grow their revenues in the shortest time possible. The results speak for themselves. (See the dealer case studies in this book.)

Another strength Jim brings to the table is that, unlike many trainers hired for flooring events, he comes from inside the flooring industry. His business, Flooring Success Systems, is dedicated solely to serving floor dealers. His Marketing Mastery Column appears in every issue of Floor Covering News, he produces and co-hosts the monthly FCNews Marketing Mastery Webinars, and he's been a featured speaker at The International Surface Events.

**For more information contact
Flooring Success Systems at
1-877-887-5791**

94

PART II

BEYOND
CORE 3

SEVEN

....

A COWBOY'S TALE

FLOOR DEALER: I keep trying to grow my business, but it never gets any bigger.

JIM: Are you fencing in, protecting, nurturing, and growing your herd of past customers?

FLOOR DEALER: I don't have time for that.

Once upon a time, long ago, there was a cowboy named Bronco Bobby who rode the range herding cattle for a living. He always worked for other ranchers; he never had a herd to call his own. One day Bronco Bobby decided, "I'm plumb tired of not having a herd to call my own." So he quit his job, used the money he'd saved to buy a small ranch with 20 head of cattle, and went into the ranching business for himself.

Bronco Bobby was determined to build the biggest cattle ranch in the territory, so year after year he worked hard buying cattle and riding the range to round up stray cows that didn't have owners. But no matter how many cows he brought back, his herd never got bigger. So Bronco Bobby worked even harder. He rode farther, roped harder, cussed louder, drew his six-gun quicker, and stayed out on the range longer than ever before. But his herd still never grew. Bronco Bobby was so discouraged that he considered selling his ranch and opening a saloon. But ranching was his dream, and the thought of giving it up made him feel lower than a snake's butt in a wagon rut.

"Ah reckon it's time to git some advice from an expert before I hang up my spurs fer good," Bronco Bobby said.

So he sent for Jimmy "Six-Gun" Augustus, the most famous cow consultant in the territory.

"Do you reckon you can help me, Jimmy Augustus?" Bronco Bobby asked when the cow consultant rode up to his ranch a few days later.

Jimmy Augustus lit up a cigar, took a long, leisurely drag, and blew a cloud of smoke into the twilight air as he eyed Bronco Bobby's teensy herd of cows.

"We'll see."

Bronco Bobby didn't see much of Jimmy Augustus over the next few days. Every now and again he'd glimpse him riding a fence line, or sitting on his horse on a ridge top, silhouetted against the sun, gazing down at Bronco Bobby's puny, pathetic herd.

About evening time a week later, Bronco Bobby was sitting on his front porch drinking coffee when Jimmy Augustus rode up out of the early-evening shadows. He dismounted, tied up his horse, and walked up to the porch, his spurs a-clinkin' with each heavy step. He leaned against a roof post, lit up a cigar, and stood puffing clouds of blue smoke as he gazed at Bronco Bobby's miserable clump of cows.

"Well?" Bronco Bobby said. "What do you think?"

The cigar tip flared red as Jimmy Augustus took a long drag. A large cloud of smoke billowed into the air.

"You've spent so much time riding out to find new cows that you've forgotten to take care of the cows you already got. That's a big mistake, one that I see a lot of ranchers make. Does it make sense to work hard getting new cows, but totally ignore the ones standing right there in front of you?"

Bronco Bobby looked thoughtful. "I reckon not."

"I've found three things you ought to be doin' to take care of yer herd. If you start doin' those three things, yer herd should grow right quick."

"Well, don't keep me in suspense! What are they?"

"First, you've got to mend yer fences. They're falling down every-where, and they've got so many dad-burn holes it's plumb amazing that every single one of yer cows hasn't wandered off."

"But, but, but ... I don't have time to mend fences, Jimmy Augustus! What with runnin' a ranch and all."

The cow consultant tipped his hat back, spat in the dust, and fixed Bronco Bobby with a steely gaze. "Boy, what's taking up all your time that's more important than keeping yer herd fenced in?"

Bronco Bobby looked chagrined.

"Second," Jimmy Augustus took a drag on his cigar and blew an extra large cloud into the chilly air, "you gotta nurture yer herd. They look like they ain't eaten in a month, ribs showin', and lookin' like they're gonna collapse at any moment. How do you expect your herd to grow if'n you don't nurture yer cows?"

Bronco Bobby hung his head, looking more ashamed than a poodle pup paddled for piddlin' in the petunias.

"Third, you got to protect them from poachers and other varmints. Three times this week yer competitor across the river snuck in like a yellow-bellied sidewinder and made off with a cow."

Bronco Bobby's head popped up. Now he looked downright mad.

Jimmy Augustus continued. "A rancher's most important job, the job he has to do before he sets out to round up new cows, is take care of the cows he's already got."

"But how can I build the biggest cattle ranch in the territory if'n I don't round up new cows?!" exclaimed Bronco Bobby.

"Boy, you don't listen too good. I didn't say not to round up new cows. I said you gotta take care of your current cows first. You gotta keep 'em fenced in, nurture 'em, and protect 'em. Otherwise roundin' up new cows is just a pure waste of time."

Bronco Bobby thought of how hard he'd worked rounding up new cows over the past couple of years, but he had nothing to show for it. His herd was no bigger than when he started.

"I reckon yer right, Jimmy Augustus."

"'Course I'm right! You fix those three things, Bronco Bobby, and I do b'lieve you'll have the biggest ranch in the territory in no time."

With that, Jimmy Augustus walked slowly back to his horse, smoke a-billowin' and spurs a-clinkin'. He mounted up and started to ride away, but before he got far he stopped and turned his horse around.

"It's good to round up new cows, Bronco Bobby, but it ain't much use if you don't take care of yer current cows. Always remember to fence, nurture, and protect yer herd."

"I will," said Bronco Bobby. "How can I ever thank you?"

"My invoice is on the kitchen table." And with that, Jimmy "Six Gun" Augustus wheeled his horse around and rode off into the sunset.

Bronco Bobby took the cow consultant's advice. He mended his fences, nurtured his herd, and protected his herd. He even challenged his cow-rustling neighbor to a gun fight at high noon. (The neighbor lost.) Within two years, just like Jimmy Augustus predicted, he had the largest ranch in the territory, with thousands and thousands of fat, happy cows that multiplied like rabbits.

And Bronco Bobby lived happily ever after.

EIGHT

....

HERD BUILDING

JIM: Your last five sales that were over $15,000 ... did they come from advertisements or referrals?

FLOOR DEALER: All referrals.

JIM: Then doesn't it make sense to build and nurture your herd so you can get the high-dollar referral business that's nearly impossible to get through advertising?

You Are A Rancher

As a floor dealer, you are a rancher. Your job is to round up a highly profitable herd of customers that you first sell to, then market to again and again for repeat and referral business.

You are not an installer, an estimator, a phone answerer, a salesperson, a warehouse manager, a bookkeeper, or any of the other tasks that go into running a flooring dealership. Even if you are currently doing some of those tasks, that is not your job description. Your job description is this: *Rancher!* (Or *Marketer.*) Your job is to round up a herd of customers, and then market to them for repeat and referral business. That is your core function. There is nothing more important. There is no higher and better use of your time. (Except maybe going fishing.)

Think about it. Installing, estimating, bookkeeping, etc., are all important to running a flooring business. But without customers there's nothing to install, nothing to estimate, and no money for a bookkeeper to manage. Your business begins and ends with getting, keeping, nurturing, and protecting your customers. Period.

I've spoken with a lot of dealers who say they "don't have time" to market to their past customers. This is like a rancher saying he doesn't have time to feed his herd or to build a fence around it.

Watch Out!

Avoid Making These Three Mistakes

Most dealers make the same three mistakes as Bronco Bobby:

1. They don't fence in their herd to keep them from wandering off.

2. They don't nurture their herd to keep them coming back and sending referrals.

3. They don't protect their herd from poachers.

These mistakes can cost you millions of dollars over the course of your career in flooring. By eliminating these mistakes you will not only reclaim those lost profits, you'll give yourself an immediate competitive advantage over other dealers.

Herd Building Principle #1:
Understand That Consumers Are Growing More Resistant To Tier 2 and Tier 3 Marketing

It's getting more and more difficult and expensive to reach cold contacts (people who don't know you, like you, or trust you) through advertising. The general public is getting ever more resistant to, and resentful of, advertising. This attitude is reflected in do-not-call lists and spam regulations. An ever-growing number of people prerecord their favorite shows, in part so they can fast-forward the commercials. On-demand sources of entertainment (Netflix, Hulu, YouTube) allow consumers to watch what they want, when they want, and virtually eliminate commercials. This trend is only going to continue.

The general public is much more suspicious than ever before. We've been lied to by politicians, Wall Street, news media, and giant corporations. We've all had the unpleasant experience of being ripped off by a company we thought we could trust.

All of this lying and cheating results in a flooring consumer who is standoffish, scared, and reluctant to trust you. You've probably noticed that over the past 10 years it's grown much more difficult to sell to prospects who visit you because they saw an ad, visited a website, or heard you on the radio. (As opposed to a repeat or referred customer.)

This does not mean you should never do Tiers 2 and 3. I teach and use these strategies myself. But if you don't have a system in place to fence, nurture, and protect your herd and the new customers you add to your herd via Tiers 2 and 3, you are increasingly putting your business at risk.

Herd Building Principle #2:
Use Permission-Based Marketing

Because of the growing resistance to Tiers 2 and 3, the race is on to build a herd of loyal customers who will buy from you over and over again, and refer others to you. The key to this is *permission-based marketing.*

When a prospect or customer gives you their contact information, either in person, over the phone, or by opting in to your website, you now have permission to communicate with them. Just make sure you follow the legal guidelines for email. (This mostly involves giving them a way to opt out. Any reputable email service has this built in to their system.)

Much more importantly, however, you now have their *emotional permission* to communicate with them. If you send them the right kind of communication, it's possible to "touch" your customers 60 or more times each year, and have them love you for it. Floor dealers I coach regularly have customers contact them when they move to give them their new mailing address. Why? So they can keep getting the dealer's mailers.

That's an absolutely amazing situation. Think about it: The last time you moved, did you contact all the companies sending you junk mail and give them your new mailing address so you could keep getting solicitations from them? Probably not.

CASE STUDY

The Ultimate "Permission" Marketing Tool!

"When my customers move, they call and give me their new address so I can keep sending them our newsletter!" —Jimmy Williams, N.C.

Think back to the last time you moved. Did you contact all the companies sending you junk mail and give them your forwarding address so they could keep sending you junk? Of course not. In fact, you probably sort your mail over a trash can and toss out *unopened* anything that even looks like junk mail. Your customers do the same thing with their junk mail, including the slick, glossy advertisements you spend thousands of dollars mailing to them.

Jimmy's customers receive the *Neighborhood Advisor™*, a turnkey, Direct Response newsletter that my team creates and sends out for our *Flooring Success Systems* members. My dealers regularly get calls from customers who have moved to give them their forwarding address so they can keep getting the newsletter! I've been using Direct Response Newsletters for almost 20 years, and I've had the same thing happen many times.

There is simply no other advertising that will do this. It doesn't exist. Period.

My dealers get stopped in grocery stores by customers telling them how much they enjoy the *Neighborhood Advisor™*. Customers walk into their stores holding the newsletter. Talk about "herd building!" Again, no other advertising can do this.

Remember! All flooring is all boring. Your newsletter should be 90% fun, valuable, entertaining content and only 10% about flooring. Otherwise it will be like those boring insurance "snooze-letters." You WILL NOT get responses like my dealers and I get. Remember this if you're creating your own newsletter.

Herd Building Principle #3:
Understand Lifetime Value Of A Customer

When building a fence around your herd, one of the first things you need to understand is *Lifetime Value of a Customer*.

Most flooring business owners and their sales people are transaction oriented. They only consider the value of a customer during that single transaction. You want to learn to be relationship oriented and understand the lifetime value of a customer.

Lifetime value is what a customer is worth to your business over the course of your relationship with them, and you should implement all your sales and marketing efforts with this concept in mind. This represents a powerful shift in thinking. Here's why:

Let's say your store's average gross revenue per transaction is $5,000. (Use your own number if $5,000 is too high or too low.) Most dealers will see a customer as worth $5,000. Here is how you should view the value of a customer over seven years:

Initial transaction:	$5,000.
Referral during that transaction:	$5,000.
Second referral during the interim 7 years	$5,000.
Second transaction (people replace flooring every 7 years on average)	$5,000.
Second referral during that transaction:	$5,000.
Lifetime Value	**$25,000.**

This doesn't include the referrals that the referrals generate, or customers who come back more often than every seven years, or people who send you more than one referral. (Or rich customers who are so tickled with their new floors that they include you in their will.) If you include all this, the true lifetime value could be as high as $50,000 to $80,000, or more. One of my *Flooring Success Systems* members got his first-ever $100,000 sale as the result of a referral. Another member landed a multistate commercial account in the high six-figures because of a referral. Therefore, each and every prospect that walks through your door is worth anywhere from $50,000 to $100,000 or more, so treat them like it.

Herd Building Principle #4:
WOW Your Customers

Wowing your customers is an important way to nurture your herd and build a fence around them from the competition. From the time a customer walks in the door, through the buying process, through the measure, through the installation, until you do the final walkthrough, you have anywhere from two weeks to two months to completely "Wow" your customer. Some of the "Wow" strategies I teach include:

- Having monitors in your showroom playing video testimonials from happy customers

- Having a *Sales Closer System* in place (see the *Design Audit*™, covered earlier) that creates total differentiation from the competition and leads prospects on a logical, step-by-step process from "shopper" to "buyer"

- Giving walk-ins a beverage menu and asking them what they'd like to drink

- Slipping on medical booties before going into a customer's house (This communicates to the customer that the dealer is careful, considerate, and will take care of the customer's home.)

- Before the installation, sending out a series of fun, entertaining "dimensional" mailers that educate the customer on the referral program, and resell them on the benefits of using that dealer

I teach many strategies for creating a "Wow" experience for the customer, which I outline in more detail in another chapter. Some dealers have said, "Why put so much effort into Wowing the customer? After all, they are there to buy flooring. I sell them flooring. That's good enough, right?"

Wrong. Unless of course you are content to have your customers see no difference between you and your competition, and you're content to sell on cheap price, and you don't care about generating repeat and referral business. If that's the case, then don't waste time Wowing your customers.

However, if you want to sell at premium prices, and if you want to maximize your repeat and referral business, and if you want to explode the size of your herd, beat the boxes, and make your competitors squawk like crows sitting on a fence, then Wowing your customers is pretty important.

Herd Building Principle #5:
Focus On Generating Referrals

Earlier I explained the *Core 3* strategy of referral marketing. Remember that word-of-mouth is the best form of marketing. Period. Here are several benefits of getting customers through referrals:

- You get customers for FREE! (No marketing costs!)

- Prospects are pre-sold! The person referring you has just told their friend or relative how utterly wonderful your business is. When they walk into your store they are more ready to buy than a cold walk-in.

- You get the halo effect. What others say about you is 100 times more effective than what you say about yourself, even if you are 100 times more eloquent.

- Very low skepticism! After all, if Aunt Rose likes your store, it must be pretty good!

- Low price resistance!

Don't miss the significance of these benefits. You are being handed a pre-sold, non-skeptical prospect who sees you with a halo and who has very little price resistance, all with no marketing costs! (Plus, referred customers are more likely to include you in their will.)

This is so powerful that you shouldn't just wait passively for referrals to happen. You need to actively seek referrals with a *Referral Marketing System*, and reward people who give them to you.

Herd Building Principle #6:
Market To Your Past Customers

Marketing to your customers does triple duty: It nurtures, protects, and fences in your herd. The vast majority of dealers do zero marketing to their past customers. The few that do mostly just send out a couple of postcards per year to their customer list, or a few emails. That's like trying to keep your herd rounded up inside a fence full of holes.

For every month that goes by that your customers don't hear from you, you lose 10% of them. After 10 months, most of them have slipped through the holes in your fence and wandered off.

That's why it's critical to market to your past customers on a monthly basis. They need to hear from you a minimum of 12 times per year. And the absolute best way to do this is with a monthly Direct Response newsletter, supplemented with a weekly e-newsletter, which will bring the total annual "touches" up to 64. (Earlier I explained why "touching" your customers up to 64 times per year is not "too much," provided you do it correctly. This mainly involves sending them fun, informative, welcome, entertaining communication that's only 10% about flooring.)

Marketing to your past customers with a Direct Response newsletter is so critical that if a gunslinger held his six-shooter to my head, cocked the hammer, and made me choose one marketing strategy to use for the rest of my life, I'd choose this one. No question. No hesitation. Why? Because I don't want to get shot! But also because a newsletter, correctly done, is one of the most powerful tools for nurturing, fencing, and protecting your herd.

Herd Building Principle #7:
Understand The True Purpose Of Tier 2
And Tier 3 Marketing

With my emphasis so far on Tier 1, it could seem like I don't be-lieve in or teach Tiers 2 and 3. It's not true. I teach dealers how to kick butt using strategies from the second and third tiers, but it's impor-tant that you understand the true purpose of doing this. There is one reason and one reason only for using Tiers 2 and 3: so you can add a new customer to your herd, and then fence them in, nurture them, and protect them. In other words, market to them forever for repeat and referral business.

Where They Eat Their Young Every Day

What The...?!

In many industries, companies break even or go into the hole to gain a new customer. All the money is made through repeat and referral business, or what's called back end.

But most dealers don't have a system in place that harvests back end, lifetime value from the new customers they bring in.

Instead, most dealers invest virtually all their time, energy, and money chasing prospects in the cold marketplace where, as my good friend Tracy Tolleson says, "They eat their young every day." They don't have their fences and feeding troughs in place so they can nurture and protect customers from the moment they are added to the herd.

12-Month Past-Customer Marketing Plan

Here's a sample marketing plan that I recommend to floor dealers I coach. These touches are NOT 100% advertising. They all use the 90/10 formula.

Marketing piece	Frequency	Total yearly touches
Newsletter (printed and mailed)	Monthly	12
e-Newsletter	Weekly	52
Birthday card (optional)	Annually	1
Thanksgiving card (optional)	Annually	1
Christmas mailer/card (optional)	Annually	1
TOTAL		**67 touches**

Some business owners wonder if 67 touches per year are too many. The answer is "it depends." If you're sending out messages that are 100% advertising (like most dealers), then yes, this is too much communication. But if you're sending out *welcome, entertaining, informative, value-added* communication (or envelopes stuffed with $100 bills), then the answer is no, this is not too much. Yes, you will have a small percentage of customers who will ask to be taken off your list. And a small percentage of those that ask to be taken off may even get a little snippy about it.

My question is: *So what?*

Don't let a tiny percentage of nagging, nit-picking, nay-saying ninnies keep you from implementing a marketing campaign that will enable you to:

- Recession-proof your business
- Create stable, predictable cash-flow

- Increase revenue

- Create sustainable, long-term growth

- Have peace of mind

- Increase customer loyalty and a sense of community with your customers

- Sink deep roots into your community and marketplace that will enable you to withstand the winds of economic turmoil

- Erect a 12-foot high, razor-topped, electrified fence around your herd, protecting them from poachers

- Be the coolest floor dealer on your block!

My dealers send monthly newsletters to lists of 500 to 5,000 contacts, and every one of them reports that only a tiny handful (usually fewer than 10) ask to be removed from the mailing list. People who ask to be removed are doing you a favor. You no longer have to waste money mailing to people who don't want to hear from you, and who are unlikely to do business with you again.

It's Time To
Stop The Madness

I've surveyed hundreds of dealers, and I always ask them two questions:

Question #1: What are you doing to promote your business?

Most common answers (90%): Newspaper, radio, TV, website, direct mail.

Question #2: What kind of results are you getting?

Most common answers (90%): *Lousy, mediocre.*

Another question I ask is if they market regularly to their past customers. Only about 2% of dealers answer "yes."

Bottom Line: The vast majority of dealers are spending thousands of dollars chasing cold prospects, but totally ignoring their past customers. Does it make any sense to invest the lion's share of your time, energy, and money into chasing strangers, yet totally ignore the only people on the planet who have proven they will buy from you? Not if you want to be a 5/45 dealer.

Be a rule breaker. Market to your past customers

NINE

....

ADVANCED
MARKETING MULTIPLIERS

FLOOR DEALER: I'd like to increase my sales by $500,000 a year within 12 months.

JIM: Then you need to view every sale not as a conclusion of a transaction, but as the starting point for multiple transactions.

FLOOR DEALER: I hadn't thought of that.

Let's take a look at how multiple strategies can be assembled together in a marketing blueprint, all reinforcing each other and creating a Marketing Multiplier effect, and giving you an enormous advantage over the boxes and other competitors.

Core 3 **Strategies (Review)**

"Core" strategy #1: *Sales Closer System.* Step-by-step, teachable, repeatable sales process that converts shoppers into buyers, and increases your closed-sale ratio, and has a huge multiplier effect on the rest of your marketing. Let's say your website generates 10 walk-ins per month, and you normally close three of them. A *Sales Closer System* can increase these to four or five closed sales. The *Sales Closer System* just multiplied the effectiveness of your website without increasing your costs.

"Core" strategy #2: *Referral Marketing System.* By using a system to farm those five website sales for immediate referral business you can add another two or three sales: also a big Marketing Multiplier.

"Core" strategy #3: *Monthly Direct Response Customer Newsletter.* If you subscribe those eight customers from your website into your monthly newsletter, you're ensuring their repeat business, and boosting your referrals over the coming months from those customers: another Marketing Multiplier.

The rest of your customer list represents a goldmine. And if you're like most dealers it's a woefully *untapped* goldmine. The monthly newsletter is hands-down the best way to mine this gold. I've worked with hundreds of dealers across the U.S. and Canada who get phenomenal results from a newsletter, many of whom have steered their businesses away from the brink of bankruptcy and into the millions-of-dollars in revenue, multiple locations, etc., with the newsletter being the principle strategy driving the turnaround.

Building On The Foundation

The Zero-Resistance Selling Environment. When customers come into your showroom, the following zero-resistance strategies are in place:

- They are handed a beverage menu and asked, "What can I get you to drink?"

- Testimonial brag wall covered with testimonials from raving-fan customers

- Monitors playing a slideshow with photos of customers, testimonials, before and after installation photos, video clips of you interviewing customers

- Cookies baked right in your store, filling it with a welcoming aroma, and served on a tray to all walk-ins

- A kid's play area with toys, video games, and DVD's

- A "Man Cave," with recliner, fridge with beers and/or sodas, large flat screen TV tuned to ESPN

This all reinforces and enhances your *Sales Closer System.*

Testimonial Drip Campaign. After the flooring is installed for each of your eight new customers, get a photo of them and a testimonial. Send postcards to the 500 homes surrounding each installation with a headline saying, "Your Neighbors On Darth Vader Drive Just Got The Beautiful Flooring Of Their Dreams!" Include the customer's name, photo, and testimonial. Include a special offer "Exclusively For Neighbors of the Pendergastmans," along with a deadline to respond. Any who respond will go through your *Sales Closer System, Referral Marketing System,* and be subscribed to your newsletter: more multiplying.

5-Around Strategy. The five homes surrounding each installation (one on either side, three across the street) get a door hanger that says, "Your Neighbors, The Pendergastmans, Just Got Gorgeous New Floors!" Include an offer with a deadline. Also include a website driving them to get your free report. Any who respond to your offer go through your *Sales Closer System, Referral Marketing System,* and are subscribed to the newsletter: more multiplying, baby!

House Party. Any customer whose sale totaled $5,000 or more (you pick the figure) gets a catered house party hosted by you! The lady of the house invites her friends over for an evening of wine and hors d'oeuvres, and to admire her new floors! You're there to meet and greet, do a raffle drawing for a free area rug, and take photos of the proceedings so you can trumpet the event in your newsletter. All attendees get a gift bag from you with gourmet coffee and chocolate, and a $200 gift certificate "Exclusively For Friends Of Rhonda Rumpelstiltskin," good for any purchase at your store of $2,500 or more. All who respond go through your *"Core 3"* strategies: 1) *Sales Closer System*; 2) *Referral Marketing System*; and 3) are subscribed to your monthly *Direct Response Customer Newsletter.*

Customer Appreciation Events. These can include holiday parties, parking lot BBQ's, wine tastings, etc. (Need more event ideas? Fellow FCNews columnist Lisbeth Calandrino has written a fun little book called *50 Events To Drive Traffic To Your Store.* Get it and I promise you'll never run out of great ideas for events. LisbethCalandrino.com) All attendees fill out raffle tickets with their name and physical and email addresses to be entered into the drawings taking place every 30 minutes. After the event, attendees are sent a "You Won!" letter, which includes a gift certificate for $200, good for any purchase of $2,500 or more. Include a deadline. All who respond go through your *Sales Closer System, Referral Marketing System,* and are subscribed to your newsletter. All who purchase go through the *5-Around Strategy*, *Testimonial Drip Campaign,* and *House Party* strategies.

Website Marketing. Here are two elements to add to your website that can dramatically enhance its effectiveness. First, have a page dedicated to testimonials. Include photos of customers whenever possible. Second, offer a free report that visitors opt in to download. This gives you the opportunity to do follow-up marketing. All opt-ins are subscribed to your newsletter. All who go from your website to visiting your store go through the *Sales Closer System* and the other multipliers mentioned above.

Facebook Testimonials. Post photos of raving-fan customers. Begin the post by saying, "Help us congratulate Bob and Betty Bugler on their new Berber!" followed by a testimonial from the Buglers, and a brief description of the floor and why they selected it. Tag them in the photo so the post appears in their timeline. When a Facebook "friend" of your customer visits your store, she goes through all the multiplier strategies.

Some dealers might say, "But, Jim! I don't have time to do all that!" If that's you, then I have a question: What is taking up all your time that's *more important* than driving sales in your business? You need to take a hard look at how you spend your workdays, and delegate a bunch of the low-dollar tasks so you can focus on activities that will propel sales and build wealth for you.

TEN

....

WHY BEING GOOD IS
NO LONGER GOOD ENOUGH

FLOOR DEALER: We provide really good service, we treat our customers right, we honor our warranties, and we never rip people off.

JIM: So what's the problem?

FLOOR DEALER: We're going broke.

Floor Dealers Have Been Sold A Bill Of Goods

"O.K., let's do a little exercise. Raise your hand if you think you offer the best flooring products and services in your town."

I was speaking to a small group of floor dealers during an intensive two-day *Marketing Mastermind Summit* I held in Las Vegas. Every hand went up. I had no way of verifying if these self-assessments by my audience members were accurate or delusions of grandeur, but that's not the point. The point is that if you ask a floor dealer if they are the best in their town you'll hardly ever hear one say, "Nah, we kind of suck." Everyone believes they're the best.

So if we have all these floor dealers providing the "best" products and services, why are so many struggling in spite of that? My years of coaching hundreds of flooring retailers has led me to the conclusion that most dealers are trying to build their businesses on ideas that are outdated, outmoded, or were never true to begin with.

I'll go even further. When it comes to figuring out how to achieve success in the flooring business, most of the advice out there is not only flat-out wrong, but will imperil your chances of success by following it. You've probably succeeded to this point *in spite of* much of the advice you've gotten from advertising reps, seminars, and industry "experts."

Truths Vs. Assumptions

At one time in history people *assumed* that the world was flat, and that the sun revolved around the Earth. People who disagreed with these assumptions and spoke out were ridiculed—even killed!—for their beliefs. But the Truth eventually won out. The *Truth* that the earth is round was proven and accepted. The *Truth* that the earth revolves around the sun was proven and accepted. The false assumptions were replaced with the Truth, and the world was changed forever.

Most dealers operate under false assumptions when it comes to building a successful business. They assume that doing a good job, or honoring their warranties, or selling top-of-the-line products, or having a slick website, or running a social media campaign is all it takes to be successful. All too often the Truth says different, and as a result they never achieve the success they want or deserve.

This is a needless tragedy for some, but a great opportunity for you. In this book you are learning *Truth* about doubling your income, eliminating stress, and living the lifestyle you truly want. Once you learn the Truth, you can dump the "assumptions" that are standing between you and success. Once you embrace the Truth, your world will change forever for the better.

Sacred Cows Make The Tastiest Hamburgers

My goal with this book is to slaughter the flooring industry's sacred cows about marketing and achieving success as a retailer. The whole herd. One by one. No mercy. No remorse. A complete bloodbath.

"Bloodbath? Geez, Jim, you sound pretty serious."

I am. I love the flooring industry; I respect the hard work and dedication that goes into building and running a dealership. Most dealers are hardworking, honorable people who want to provide good service to their customers. So I hate it when I see so many of them struggling needlessly because of bad information and industry myths.

13 Flooring Industry Myths That Sabotage Dealers' Success

1. You've got to run your ads over and over again to see results.

2. Provide great customer service and/or the latest brand-name products and your business will thrive (aka, the "build a better mousetrap" theory).

3. You have to spend a lot of money to effectively market your flooring business.

4. You've got to be "competitive" in your pricing (i.e., sell on low price), especially in a slow market or in the presence of a big-box store.

5. You've got to "get your name out there" and build up "name recognition" and "brand yourself" in order to succeed.

6. Ad reps give good marketing advice; you should listen to them.

7. Having a "professional looking" website, or being on Facebook, LinkedIn, Twitter, etc., will automatically generate sales.

8. Frequent marketing will offend prospects and drive away business.

9. Building up a successful floor dealership is all about luck.

10. Building up a successful floor dealership is all about spending years working 60-70 hours per week, sacrificing my family, my friends, my life.

11. I can't charge premium prices. I live in _____ (big city, small town, East Coast, West Coast, in the middle, etc.) and the customers here only care about one thing: cheap price.

12. Marketing doesn't work. I've tried it before and it just wasted my money.

13. It's impossible to build an *Ideal Business*, live an *Ideal Lifestyle*, generate real wealth, and have a stress-free, rewarding career in the flooring business.

This is B.S. of the highest and purest quality, acceptable as fertilizer for even the most discriminating of organic farmers. Throughout the pages of this book I systematically dismantle every one of these myths. You're meeting other floor dealers, just like you, who once struggled but who now are prospering in large part because they have unshackled themselves from these myths and have learned new ways of thinking about and promoting their businesses.

Build a better mousetrap and the world will beat a path to your door ... yeah, right.

This is one of the biggest misconceptions in the floor covering business. In today's incredibly competitive, hectic world, nobody's beating a path to anyone's door. Some of the "best," most knowledgeable, most technically skilled dealers spend year after year struggling, stressed out, stuck in the same place, and never able to take their business to the next level. This is because even if you are highly skilled at the technical aspects of flooring, if you don't have a system that generates a steady flow of new, good customers, you will always struggle, experience limited growth, and maybe even go out of business altogether. Yet many dealers think that just because they have great skills and great products and great customer service that they will have success. That their business will grow and they will make a lot of money. That people will beat a path to their door. I call this the *"build a better mousetrap"* theory, and it's totally false. Building wealth in the flooring business, beating the boxes, and totally dominating your market is not about how much you know about floor covering. It's about how much you know about marketing systems. (See "Marketing Systems" definition in Jim's Lexicon.)

Anyway, the only way you are going to make a lot of money is if you can fill your showroom continuously, and predictably, with prospects who are willing to pay you top dollar and not even think about shopping with your competitors. (Or if you run a mobile showroom, to get your phone to ring continuously and predictably with highly qualified prospects.) Your skill in the floor covering business (by itself) won't accomplish this. If you don't combine your technical skills with the right kind of marketing skills, your business is destined to either fail or wallow in mediocrity, and you will never make the kind of money you want or deserve, you'll certainly never dominate your market, and the boxes will beat *you*.

The hard, cold fact of life is that the person who has learned the secrets of powerful, effective *marketing systems* is the one who will always make the most money, regardless of their skills.

I know this isn't fair ...

- The dealers who have the best installers, and who are the best at customer service, and who honor their warranties should automatically make the most money. But they don't.

- People should beat a path to the door of the best store. But they don't. (Case in point: Pay attention to how many cars are filling up Home Depot's parking lot next time you drive by. Many of those are *your* prospects and customers. Ouch.)

- People should realize that installations aren't "Free," no matter what the box stores claim. But they don't.

- People should see that a quality installation by a trained craftsman is a critical part of flooring, equally as important as the product itself, and should be happy to pay for it. But they don't. (They want it "Free.")

- People should only seek out the most highly skilled and ethical dealers, and happily pay top dollar. But they don't.

- People should realize that box stores and all those sleazy, bait-and-switch "discount" dealers offer those super-low prices, and "Free" installations, just to bamboozle customers. But they don't.

- I wish the real world worked like that. But it doesn't.

- It's not fair. But who said life is fair? (If you're looking for "fair," you are looking in the wrong place. It should be apparent by now that I'm not going to give you "fair," I'm going to give you the truth. Even if it's tough to hear.)

Please don't misunderstand me. Providing great service and being technically skilled are a prerequisite to success. You can't succeed without these elements in place. *They just aren't enough anymore.*

Let me repeat that because it's important: **They aren't enough anymore.**

Maybe this hurts your feelings. But I'm not saying this to make you feel good. I'm saying this to give you the opportunity to learn how to make lots of money, and to help you achieve not just financial freedom, but total financial and business autonomy. And that should make you feel fantastic. So I've got to give it to you straight. I think you are man or woman enough to take it. You can fight this fact and struggle, stagnate, or even go broke. Or you can change—embrace this radically new concept and experience dramatic increases in your income and improvements in your lifestyle. By making this giant, mental paradigm shift, you'll instantly gain an enormous competitive advantage over everybody else in your area. And you'll take a big step closer toward achieving your *Ideal Business, Ideal Lifestyle*™. Understanding this concept is the foundation to sound thinking about the marketing of your business.

Achieve Your *Ideal Business, Ideal Lifestyle*™

The purpose of your business: to fund and facilitate your *Ideal Lifestyle*.

I was doing a private coaching call with a floor dealer from North Carolina. He told me that he made a personal salary of over $400,000 a year from his flooring business. His biggest challenge was not making more money (though increasing the size of his business was one of his goals); his biggest challenge was having a life *outside* of business. He was working 60-70 hours per week, including weekends; not able to spend enough time with his daughters; never able to take a vacation. He was what I call a "successful slave."

With a little coaching I was able to help him immediately free up an extra day per week to enjoy himself, and to set him on a course to achieve even more freedom to pursue what had meaning, purpose, and value for him outside of his flooring dealership. He sent me an email a few months later thanking me, and telling me about a vacation to Disney World he was able to take with his family. It was his first vacation in years.

I believe and teach that the true purpose of your flooring business is to *fund and facilitate your Ideal Lifestyle*. I feel so strongly about this concept that the name of the monthly newsletter my company publishes for dealers in my coaching program is called *Ideal Business, Ideal Lifestyle*™. I've even trademarked the phrase. All the sales and marketing strategies in this book have been engineered with this end in mind: *to help you build your Ideal Business so you can live your Ideal Lifestyle*.

Too many dealers work too hard for too little, putting in 50, 60, or 70+ hours per week. Many of those who *do* make an excellent income are frustrated because they feel chained to their stores. (The "Successful Slave" syndrome.)

My sincere desire is to help you achieve your *Ideal Business, Ideal Lifestyle*™. Let's face it; you could have gotten a 9-5 job, worked the corporate "rat race," but instead you chose to be an entrepreneur. And you did it (at least in part) because in the flooring business you saw a better opportunity to achieve your dreams and goals than in working for someone else. And this boils down to the two things that almost every dealer wants from their business: *Time & Money*.

But most dealers feel like they spend too much time working, and they feel like they don't make enough money.

And that's why I've written this book. I want you to learn how you can achieve the dreams and the goals that motivated you to operate your own dealership; how to replace common flooring industry myths that are holding you back with truths that will unleash your potential; how to make more *money* than you ever dreamed possible (regardless of where you live), and have the *time* to enjoy it.

In short, to achieve your *Ideal Business* and live your *Ideal Lifestyle*.

ELEVEN

....

WHY TRADITIONAL ADVERTISING STINKS LIKE A SACK OF DEAD FISH

JIM: So, how much are you spending on advertising?

FLOOR DEALER: $4,000 per month.

JIM: What kind of results are you getting?

FLOOR DEALER: *Lousy.*

"The Crowd Is Always Wrong"

That's a quote by Earl Nightingale, and it's an axiom by which I build my business and live my life. It's a principle I pound home relentlessly to the floor dealers I coach. (Along with the principle "Try to avoid smoking in your customer's home.") Before we get into the meat-n-potatoes of this chapter, I want to illuminate this principle's importance to your success.

My surveys of hundreds of dealers across the U.S. and Canada reveal that the vast majority of them use identical, "traditional" advertising methods. My surveys also reveal that most dealers using these methods are getting lousy to mediocre results. This means that every year, untold millions of advertising dollars are wasted because dealers follow the crowd.

(Advertising isn't the only area in which dealers copy each other's ineffective business-building methods. Throughout this book I cover other success-sabotaging "crowd" behaviors common to the flooring industry, and how you can replace them with *success* behaviors.)

The 80/20 Rule

20% of businesses in any industry make 80% of the money, with everyone else fighting for the scraps. This is definitely true in the flooring business. If you want to be part of the 80% fighting over the scraps left by the more successful dealers, it's not hard: Just follow the crowd.

How Floor Dealers Follow The Majority

- They use Name, Rank, and Serial Number ads.
- They talk about features, not benefits.
- They don't answer the unspoken question on every consumer's mind: *why should I buy flooring from you instead of your competitors?*
- They don't educate their prospects.
- They compete on price.

- The inside of their installation vans have layers of grime dating back to the Mesozoic period.

My goal is to give you strategies that will help you be different from other dealers. Don't worry about breaking with the business norm. Don't worry if "no one else is doing it." Instead, see this as a sign that you're on the right path; the path leading *away* from the crowd; the path leading to success.

I'll take this idea further. You should *try* to do things outside of the business norm. *Seek out* ways to be different. (Reading this book is a great place to start!) If other dealers are doing something one way, figure out a way to do it differently. This will cause you to stand out and will ensure that you are not bumbling down the same dead-end path as the mediocre majority.

 **Be Different**

It always amuses me when dealers tell me they want to create differentiation, but then are stubbornly resistant to doing anything different from industry norms.

Now hear this! If you want to create differentiation, you've got to do things ... (*drum roll, please*) ... DIFFERENTLY! You should look for ways to break industry norms, to do things differently than everyone else. If you catch yourself or an employee or a sales rep saying, "But that's not how it's done," good! You're probably on the right track!

- Answer the phones differently
- Dress differently
- Market differently
- Price differently (Don't price cheaper, price *differently*)
- Sell differently
- Conduct consultations differently
- Etc.

Problems With "Traditional" Advertising

There are two ways to market your business. One way is with "traditional" image advertising, also known as institutional advertising. The other is with Direct Response Marketing, which is the method I teach. Knowing the difference between the two is critical to your success. (Almost as critical as training your installers not to ask your customers' daughters out on dates.) Since very few dealers know how to use Direct Response, most wind up using "traditional" advertising.

You need to get your name out there.

How many times have you heard an ad rep or a web designer or a flooring industry "expert" say this? How many times have *you* said it?

Here's another one you may have heard: *Prospects need to see your message 7 times before they'll respond.*

This is the thinking behind "traditional," "institutional," "brand building" types of advertising. The idea is that you put your business name out there over and over again trying to build up "name recognition." If enough people see your name enough times, hopefully some of them will visit your store or call you. There is a grain of truth to this. You can get some new customers by putting your name out there over and over again. But there are four huge problems with trying to increase your revenue by building up name recognition.

Problem #1: It's very expensive.

Let's say you live in a small town with 60,000 people. How much do you think it will cost for ads, radio spots, billboards, websites, SEO, and other media to saturate your market sufficiently to build up name recognition? A quarter-million dollars invested over a number of years would be a conservative figure, and this is for a very small market. Giant corporations like Home Depot or Lowe's can afford to saturate a market (nationally and locally) with enough ads to build up name recognition. Most dealers can't afford this.

Problem #2: There's a tremendous amount of waste.

Again, let's say you have a market with 60,000 people. Most of them don't need flooring on any given day. With a "traditional," market-saturation type of approach, you're paying to have your message seen by tens-of-thousands of people who are not in the market to buy flooring. Again, giant corporations can afford to dump money into advertising methods that produce mountains of waste, but most dealers can't.

Problem #3: It takes a long, long time to work.

Even with a gigantic advertising budget, how long do you think it will take to build up sufficient name recognition with 60,000 people that it translates into meaningful sales figures? Two years? Three? And who has a gigantic ad budget? Certainly not most floor dealers. A more realistic time frame, based on the financial resources of most dealers, is roughly until the next ice age. Can you afford to wait until North America is covered in a sheet of ice for your advertising strategy to work? Most can't.

Problem #4: You have to be number one (or close to it).

In order for a "brand building" or "name recognition" strategy to be most effective, your dealership's name has to be among the first that the majority of the people in your market think of when anyone says the word "flooring."

Ask 100 people at random in your market area who they think of when you say the word "flooring." If most of them name a business other than yours (including Home Depot, Lowe's, or Empire), then you've basically lost the "name recognition" game. This is why big companies totally saturate markets with their name using a variety of media including TV, radio, internet, direct mail, billboards, etc. This game basically boils down to dollars: Whoever can throw the most money at it usually wins. For this reason, it's next to impossible for a local dealer to beat the box stores in the "name recognition" or "brand building" game. (There *are* other ways to beat them, and beat them badly, which I cover in this book.) Even if there are no big boxes in your area, you still have to outspend all your competitors to a point where you are at or near the top of the list in name recognition in order to get the biggest benefits from this strategy.

Even outspending your competitors doesn't always guarantee that you'll get high rankings in name recognition. You can have a small competitor who doesn't spend a dime on advertising, but who has been located on the busiest street in town for 20 years. Since for decades everyone has seen his sign every time they drive by, you could spend $100,000 a year and still not knock him out of the top "name recognition" slot. (Arrg!)

Right now you might be saying, "O.K., Jim, I realize that trying to build up name recognition in my market is super expensive and that it may take years for my business to reach the top slot in people's minds, if it ever does. But I still need to advertise so I can get more customers." Great! Start with the *Core 3* strategies I covered earlier (Tier 1). Don't move on to Tiers 2 and 3 until your Tier 1 is completely up and running.

In this book I cover effective Direct Response Marketing methods from Tier 2 and Tier 3 that will produce results quickly. But if you're doing the type of advertising that 98% of floor dealers use, you're not going to get the results you are looking for. Traditional, brand-building types of ads usually do nothing but suck money out of dealers' wallets like a turbo-charged, industrial Hoover vacuum, and give little to nothing in return. (Except the deep, personal satisfaction of knowing that you are helping your local ad rep make his Lexus payments.)

This is because these kinds of ads have serious problems ...

Why Traditional Ads And Websites Don't Work

Traditional Ads & Websites Copy The Copycats

Almost all flooring ads and websites use the *Name, Rank, and Serial Number* formula: business name at the top, bullet points of products (sometimes with teaser prices), and contact information. Google "flooring" in your city and pull up the websites of three of your competitors and you'll see that virtually all of them are using this formula. Pull up *your* website: odds are you are, too. You might see cosmetic differences in color and graphics, some will have different products than others, but there is no substantive difference in the message of most websites. This same formula is used in newspaper ads, inserts, direct mail, and on and on. If you are using these kinds of ads, you are creating absolutely no differentiation from the competition.

Traditional Ads & Websites Fail To Answer The Unspoken Question On Every Prospect's Mind

Put yourself in your prospect's shoes. She doesn't know anything about flooring, and she doesn't have a relationship with any dealers, so she goes to the internet and does a search for "Flooring Boston" to find information about retailers in her area. She sees site after site, each using the *Name, Rank, and Serial Number* formula. She is desperately searching for an answer to the unspoken question on her mind: *"Why should I do business with you versus every competitive option available to me, including doing nothing?"* Unfortunately, none of them answer this question. (IMPORTANT! Extensive market testing has shown that offers of "free hugs with every installation" are not an effective answer to the "why should I buy from you" question.)

Open up your website, or any ads you've run in the past year. Now ask yourself, "Based on the strength of these ads, why should my prospects choose me instead of my competitors? What *concrete reasons* have I provided them to give their money to *me* instead of to Lowe's, Home Depot, Empire, or any of the other floor retailers they have access to, locally or online?" If your ad does not give a clear, compelling, easily understood answer, then you're opening yourself up to the next problem.

Traditional Ads & Websites Cause Dealers To Compete On Price

If you've copied the other dealers by using the *Name, Rank, and Serial Number* formula for your ads and website, if you've failed to answer the unspoken question on your prospect's mind, if you've failed to create differentiation between you and your competition, then your prospects are going to make their choice on the only criteria they have left: *price*. (Or whichever dealer offers them free beer.)

This is not your prospect's fault. If you are one of five dealers in her area and none of you differentiate yourselves, as far as she is concerned you're all selling the same thing. It may not be true: There may be radical differences between the dealers, their level of service, their warranties, their products, their expertise. But the advertising all of you are using does not convey these differences, so in her mind you're all the same. Only an idiot would pay more when she can get the same thing for less down the street. Imagine going to your grocer and seeing two displays of oranges. They all look the same; no differentiation. However, the first group is priced at $0.50 each, but the second group is priced at $1.00 each. Which would most people buy? Absent any kind of education as to why the higher priced group is more expensive and why it's worth the extra money, the lower priced group is going sell much better. It doesn't matter that the higher priced oranges are organic, that they taste better, have more vitamins, and no pesticide residue. No one knows this because the advertising created no differentiation.

For all of these reasons, most floor dealers who succeed do so *in spite* of their efforts in "traditional" advertising, not because of it. So why do so many dealers burn mountains of cash on advertising that doesn't produce the results they are looking for? For three reasons:

First, most dealers don't know how to effectively promote their business. As I said earlier, knowing the technical aspects of running a flooring business and knowing how to market that business are two completely different skill sets. Just because you know how to do one does not mean you know how to do the other.

Second, it's human nature to copy those around us. We've all watched movies where someone at a fancy dinner party, obviously out of their element, is faced with a bewildering assortment of silverware on either side of their plate. When the first course is served, what do they do? They sneak peeks to either side to see what everyone else is doing. Most of us have done the same thing in various situations: when we go to a new school, visit a new church, or join a new health club. We look at what everyone else is doing to get cues to how we should behave. This natural human tendency can be helpful in certain situations, but when it comes to advertising our flooring business it can be deadly. It turns into a case of the blind-and-dumb leading the blind-and-dumb. If you're not careful you might follow someone right over a cliff.

Third, dealers have been misled. The flooring industry is a culture that preaches the gospel of "brand building" with the fervor of a charismatic evangelist. Many accept on faith that brand building, or building up name recognition, is an effective advertising strategy for a local dealer. Unfortunately, in the vast majority of cases this is a terrible approach for dealers because to effectively build up the brand of your store requires a tremendous amount of time and money. Most succeed *in spite* of efforts in that direction, not because of them.

The Antidote To Traditional Advertising: *Direct Response Marketing*

The alternative to traditional "brand building" advertising is Direct Response Marketing. Here's a brief explanation. With traditional advertising you put ads out over and over again and hope that if enough people see your ad enough times that it will eventually translate into more sales. Direct Response Marketing compels prospects to take action right now. Done correctly, you can put an ad or a letter out on Monday and be making sales by Friday. It also answers the unspoken question on every consumer's mind: *Why should I do business with you instead of your competitors?* A happy side benefit of Direct Response Marketing is that over time you *will* build up name recognition. Two birds, one very effective stone.

What
The...?!

Be Personal, Not "Corporate"

As a small business, you have many advantages that the boxes don't, most notably the ability to be extremely personal with your customers, both in your marketing and when you meet them in person. Large corporations are forced to do dozens of things that the general public finds annoying or downright hates. Things like sounding "corporate" and impersonal in their advertising, treating people like numbers, and abusing their customers with phone menu systems. ("Press 1 to be put on hold indefinitely; press 2 to be connected with a bored, underpaid, unmotivated, untrained customer service representative; press 3 to be accidentally disconnected; press 4 to hear these options again.") They do this not because it makes them more money, but because they are large, bloated bureaucracies and they think they have no choice.

What I find tragically amusing is when a small business owner who does NOT have to do these things—who has the powerful marketing opportunity to be extremely personal with their prospects and customers both in person and in their marketing—attempts to sound like a big "professional" corporation by using phone menus and other annoying things. Dumb, dumb, dumb.

I mentioned earlier that there are ways to beat the big boxes. This is one of those ways. Seek out ways to create a personal experience with your customers. Make them feel special. Build a relationship. People want to do business with people, not with big, impersonal corporations.

The Myth Of The Silver Bullet

In werewolf lore, there is only one way to kill a beast that transforms from man to wolf: Shoot it with a silver bullet. It seems that every werewolf movie climaxes with the hero, gun in hand, hunting (or being hunted by) the monster, hoping for the chance to make that one critical shot and rescue the villagers from the nightmare that's been terrorizing them for generations. Yes, if you want to rid your village of a werewolf, there's really only one option available to you: a silver bullet, baby.

Unfortunately, too many dealers believe something similar about the "not-enough-customers" werewolf. They desperately search for that one "magic" advertising solution that's going to create a bunch of walk-in traffic, make them a ton of money, and solve all their financial woes; that one strategy that's going to kill the "werewolf" and rid their business of the financial nightmare that's been terrorizing them. I call this the "Myth of the Silver Bullet." Well, outside of werewolf movies, there are no silver bullets. (Sorry.) Marketing *systems*, not silver bullets, are the key to creating a highly profitable flooring business, and slaying the hairy, scary, financial werewolf once and for all. And the *Core 3* is a powerful and critical marketing *system* to have in place.

Marketing System = A set of interconnected sales and marketing strategies working together to create the Marketing Multiplier effect, create differentiation, reduce price-resistance, and generate sales. Each strategy in a marketing system compounds the effectiveness of every other strategy. The whole is far more powerful than the sum of its parts.

Watch Out!

Don't Grow Overly Dependent Upon A Single Source Of New Customers!

If you have a marketing strategy or a source that's generating a large percentage of your new customers, be careful. What happens if this source dries up? A number of years ago I learned this lesson the hard way. I was getting about 30% of my new customers from a single campaign I was rolling out to different neighborhoods. Almost overnight it stopped working. Ouch. Fortunately I had other marketing funnels in place, (including the *Core 3*) that filled the gap until I was able to replace the no-longer-working campaign.

Dealers Are Saying Good-Bye To "Traditional" Advertising Forever

Remember, "traditional" or institutional advertising is all about putting your name out there over and over again to build up "name recognition." This takes a long, long time to work, it's extremely expensive, and there is a ton of waste.

Direct Response Marketing is the other method of marketing, and is the one I teach. Done correctly, it compels prospects and customers to take action right now, immediately. It's also cheaper and works much faster, so it's a much more effective and appropriate technique for local dealers.

It's possible to use either "traditional" advertising or Direct Response Marketing with any of the three tiers of marketing. I teach dealers to use Direct Response for all three tiers.

This is an important distinction to make because some dealers think I'm against using Tiers 2 and 3. Not true! I teach dealers how to use Direct Response methods for all three tiers. What I'm against is throwing away money year-after-year on traditional, "brand building" methods that aren't working, regardless of the tier in which they are used.

Most of my dealers don't do "traditional," brand-building advertising at all anymore. Zero. None. Some don't even do Tier 2 and Tier 3 marketing, choosing to focus primarily on Tier 1. Their businesses are exploding by using these Tier 1/*Core 3* strategies.

How would you feel having a business that's growing by leaps and bounds, and it's doing so with 80%-90% repeat and referral customers? You and your sales team would have a much easier, more pleasant, more profitable job selling, that's for sure. Not to mention the king's ransom you'd save on advertising costs. This savings alone will give you a huge advantage over your competitors who continue to throw money away on useless, copycat advertising.

This is exactly what happened to Tim, a floor dealer from Minnesota ...

CASE STUDY

How Tim Began Pocketing An Extra $15,000-$20,000 Per Month!

Tim Rea was spending $15,000-$20,000 per month on traditional newspaper and radio advertising. The problem was most of the people who came in from these ads were price shoppers, so he had to sell three times as much to make the same profit. Now all that has changed. Because of the strategies he's implemented, he was able to stop all traditional advertising. By using the systems you're learning in this book, he was able to make the shift to 100% referral and repeat customers. "Since I quit advertising, my sales are up this year over last year," Tim told me. "Plus my margins are a lot higher because I'm not attracting price shoppers anymore. I'm also saving the $15k-$20k I was spending on newspaper and radio."

Tim had switched to doing mostly Tier 1/*Core 3* marketing. I've worked with a number of dealers who have made this switch. Remember, I'm all for using Tiers 2 and 3 provided they're done with Direct Response strategies. However, it does illustrate the power of Tier 1/*Core 3*, and that you should have those strategies in place before moving on to the other tiers.

TWELVE

....

UNFAIR ADVANTAGE MARKETING THAT BREAKS ALL THE RULES

FLOOR DEALER: But nobody in the flooring business does what you're suggesting I do!

JIM: That's the point.

Steve was standing in his Arizona flooring store when a man walked in holding a letter.

"My neighbor said I should come and see you," the man said, handing the letter to Steve. He recognized it as one of the direct mail pieces he had sent out the week before. "You sent this to my neighbor, and when he found out I was planning to have tile installed in my house, he brought this over to me and said 'You've gotta go see Steve.'"

The letter was not your typical flooring ad. I know, because I wrote it. It was four pages long, crammed full of text, written in 11-point font, black print on white paper, and no photos or mention of any flooring products whatsoever. Yet they generated an 11-1 return on investment, Steve later told me.

To make the situation even more remarkable, the letter had not been sent to the tile customer, but to his neighbor. "When was the last time you got a piece of 'junk mail' from a business, and were so excited about it you walked it over to your neighbor and told them they just had to contact the company in the ad?" Steve asked me.

Never.

That's the power of Direct Response Marketing. Conventional advertising wisdom says that you can't sell flooring with a four-page letter with no photos or description of products; that you need lots of color and graphics; that you shouldn't be too wordy; that you need lots of white space.

Hogwash. Hundreds of savvy floor dealers who have used the Direct Response Marketing strategies I teach have proven differently. What you need is marketing that doesn't bore prospects, but instead grabs their attention, develops interest, heightens desire, and compels them to take action. But as I've said before, most flooring ads and websites are about as compelling as a fistful of Sleep-Eze.

So what are the elements that go into a compelling marketing piece? Here are a few of the most important:

Benefits. Your prospect only cares about three things: benefits, benefits, benefits. Everybody's favorite radio station is W.I.I.F.M: *What's In It For Me?* Your business name, your slogan, or how many years you've been in business are not seen by your prospects as benefits. Your ads need to educate the prospect on the actual, real, *demonstrable* benefits of buying from you versus from your competitors.

"Cheap price" doesn't count as a benefit because almost everyone says it, it requires no sales or marketing imagination, and it attracts pesky, hard-to-eradicate critters (also known as "price shoppers") to your business.

Testimonials. What others say about you is 100 times more effective than what you say about yourself, even if you are 100 times more eloquent.

Unique Selling Proposition. Most floor dealers use Universal Selling Propositions like "Number One In Customer Satisfaction," "Free Estimates, Guaranteed Lowest Price," and "How Boring Can We Be And Still Stay In Business?" A good USP focuses like a laser beam on a specific, concrete benefit that is unique to your business, or is perceived as unique by your prospects.

Write like you talk. In your marketing and advertising, use conversational language that relates to your prospect and sounds like a real, live human being. Don't use advertise-ese: *"Our Goal At* Boring Flooring *Is To Provide Our Customers With Superior Floors And Stellar Service As We Strive To Make The World A Better Place One Floor At....A... Ti...."*

(Zzzzzz...MMzzzz... Huh? What? Oops, sorry. Even *writing* in advertise-ese puts me to sleep.)

Your prospects don't talk that way, so you shouldn't either.

Why The Marketing I Use And Teach
"Looks" Different

Remember what Earl Nightingale said: *The crowd is always wrong.* Because of this I never emulate the masses, especially when it comes to marketing. The marketing strategies I teach and use are not about copying the "slick," impersonal, institutional, corporate-type advertising you see floor dealers using everywhere.

Depending upon which study you read, the average person is bombarded with 3,000-10,000 advertising messages a day. The human mind simply cannot absorb this much input, so people have developed advertising filters that screen out all that clutter. These filters act like the pop-up blockers on your computer. You want to use marketing that's specifically engineered to cut through the clutter, get past that marketing filter, and get noticed. You want your marketing to grab your prospect by the lapels, shake them out of their lethargy, and *compel them* to pay attention. You *will not* command their attention using a "slicker" four-color brochure, or brighter newspaper insert, or fancier flyer, or by adding more bells-and-whistles to your website. Here's one reason why:

Think back to how many times you have driven through your town, got to where you were going, but didn't even notice all the slick, colorful, flashing business signs all along the way. You didn't notice because your advertising filter was up and you blocked them all out. But then you round a corner in your neighborhood and something catches your eye; you actually turn your head to look. You see an ugly, handwritten cardboard sign nailed to a telephone pole advertising a garage sale. That ugly, hand-written cardboard sign did what all those slick, expensive, professional signs couldn't: It got past your advertising filter.

Your marketing has one critical job: to get past your prospect's advertising filter and get them to buy your products. The strategies I teach and use are not about logos, ego, looking fancy or slick, or appearing "professional." On the list of priorities, all of those things are a distant second to cutting through the jungle of distractions entangling your prospects, and compelling them to contact you and buy from you.

Why Direct Response Marketing Works

I want you to get a very clear picture in your mind. Imagine a weary mom sprawled out on the couch, exhausted after schlepping three loud, energetic kids to school, soccer, and music lessons. Let's call her Jane. When Jane got home she tossed her keys on the counter somewhere, sent the kids out to play, put on some sweats, and now she's finally got a few minutes to herself. She's watching her favorite show on TV, bag of chips and glass of wine within easy reach. Can you picture her? Can you see Jane clearly?

Alright. Your mission is to create a marketing message that's so compelling that you can get Jane to jump up from the couch, change back into her nice clothes, find her keys, get the kids back in the car, and drive to your store. Because if you can get *Jane* to respond, you can get *anyone* to respond.

Direct Response Marketing is the way to do this. *Direct Response* gives potential customers a strong message that compels them to run to the phone and call you immediately, or get their butt off the couch and drive across town to your store. You put the ad out, and you get a direct response back from the prospect. *Direct Response* is tough-minded, results-driven marketing that can be tracked. A good direct marketer insists that if you put one dollar into an ad, that you get more than a dollar back, plus a new customer. If you can't track the results, and if you don't get immediate response, it's not *Direct Response Marketing*.

I recommend that you go on a strict, direct marketing diet for the next six months. Stop all marketing that is not Direct Response, and cannot be held accountable for its success. (In other words, marketing that cannot be tracked.)

Done properly, a good Direct Response campaign will bring you immediate sales. It will enable you to put an ad out on Monday and start making sales from the ad by Friday. Even faster if you do a Direct Response email campaign to the right contact list. (I'm not talking about email spamming, but marketing to a list of people who have given you permission to email them.) This is very powerful. With most traditional advertising, business owners put out an ad over and over again, and hope and pray that it will somehow, *someday* translate into a sale. They have no way to predict or establish a track record for the success or failure of any ad campaign.

What would it be worth to you to know that you could put out an ad on Monday, and know with reasonable certainty that you would be making money on that ad by Friday? And not just making money, but creating a predictable, constant flow of cash? This is exactly what Direct Response Marketing allows you to do. And this is what I've been teaching dealers to do successfully for years.

Direct Response Marketing Will Build Up Your Brand

I've said a lot about why "traditional," brand-building types of advertising are not very effective for local flooring retailers, in part because this kind of approach is expensive and takes a long time to work. However, a happy side benefit of Direct Response Marketing is that you *will* build up name recognition; you *will* build your brand. And you'll likely do it a lot more quickly than with "traditional" advertising methods.

Sales Letters

For direct mail marketing, I teach dealers to use very personal-looking-and-sounding sales letters rather than slick, four-color "corporate" pieces. This has several advantages:

1. It automatically looks different from everyone else's.

2. It's very personal. It looks like you wrote them a personal letter on your computer and sent it to them. People don't want to do business with a corporation; they want to do business with a real, live, flesh-and-blood human being. Think about your customer who has to deal every day with faceless, non-caring corporations. Every day people call big companies on the phone and get dumped into automated menus where they hear *"Press one to be on hold forever; press two to be accidentally disconnected; press three to speak with a robotic, disinterested, bored, unmotivated member of our staff who doesn't care about you; press four to hear these options again."*

3. Changes are easy. If you need to tweak your marketing message, no problem. If you need to create a campaign to take advantage of a local news item or event, it's easy to do. Full-color brochures and ad campaigns are expensive and can take months to roll out. I've gotten so good at sales letters that I can have an idea on Monday and have the campaign out by Wednesday or Thursday, and you can learn to do the same.

4. It's way less expensive!

The More You Tell, The More You Sell

Most of the sales letters I use myself and provide to floor dealers are anywhere from 2 to 20 pages long. People tell me all the time, "No one will read a long sales letter." Many years ago I used to own a carpet cleaning company. I created a four-page sales letter with 10-point font, crammed full of text, with no photos or fancy graphics. Just a letter. Ever seen a four-page letter selling carpet cleaning? Neither had the printer. When I took it into the print shop their graphic designer very tactfully said, "Boy, that's an awful lot of words." Thankfully I knew enough about marketing to ignore her. That sales letter generated tens-of-thousands of dollars.

Most ad agencies and ad salesmen will tell you to use as few words as possible. They want you to buy the biggest ad you can possibly afford, use a lot of color, put your logo at the top, and leave a lot of empty space. These ads look extremely slick and professional; they just don't work very well.

Your ads, letters, and websites are salesmanship in print

Can you imagine sitting face to face with a prospect who is interested in flooring, and limiting yourself to only 50 words? After you spoke 50 words, you could not say anything else. No matter if the prospect had questions, was ready to buy, or wanted more information. You had to stop at 50 words. INSANE. It makes no sense. Yet dealers do this all the time with their advertising. They don't realize that these ads are their salesmen. They send out hundreds of printed "salesmen" and limit them to only a few words, a catchy logo, and a phone number.

I think the mistake is made in part because dealers try to use their marketing pieces to reach people who aren't interested in flooring. They think, "If I keep the ad short, the people who aren't interested will be able to read it quickly and not get bored. Then maybe they'll decide to visit my store."

Whatever the reasoning, it's a mistake. You cannot reach people who have zero interest in flooring. So quit trying. Your job is to target people who have some level of interest, and get them to buy from *you* instead of your competitors.

Someone who *is not* interested in flooring won't read 10 words about the subject. A person who *is* interested will read 10 pages. Think about the last time you bought a car, booked a vacation, bought a computer (or purchased a private island). How much time did you spend researching and reading about it? I'll wager that you read more than just a handful of words on a postcard. You likely spent hours reading through ads and websites. Why? Because this decision was important to you and you wanted to make the best choice possible.

Put yourself in the place of the average flooring consumer. They know nothing about flooring. When they decide to begin looking for new floors, they have no idea which product to choose, which dealer is best, what to look for. They are clueless. On top of that, flooring is a big-ticket item that can run into the tens-of-thousands of dollars. Plus it's a decision they'll have to live with for a long, long time. They want to get it right. They are craving information. If you are the one to give them the information they need, and educate them on how to choose a flooring dealership, how to avoid common pitfalls, and the benefits of working with your dealership, you will be light years ahead of your competition. They will gladly read as much information as you give them. Even if it's four pages with no pictures. Unless you are boring. If your ads, letters, and websites are boring, no one will read them. So make sure your marketing isn't boring. Give lots and lots of benefits to your prospects.

By the way, the dealers I coach use a 25-page educational sales letter called *The Consumer's Guide To Floor Covering*. Not only do their customers read it front to back, they come back to the store thanking the dealers and raving about how helpful it was, and wind up purchasing.

The More You Tell, The More You Sell

Using the Direct Response strategies covered in this chapter and the next, I wrote a sales letter for floor dealers that's four pages long, with 12-point, New Roman font, no photos (other than a photo of the dealer on the first page), black-and-white printing on plain white paper, and absolutely no mention of specific flooring products. I instruct dealers to mail it in a plain, white envelope with no business information on the outside.

According to advertising "experts" this letter shouldn't work for a number of reasons:

- It's too long. No one will read that many words.
- There's no white space.
- There are no photos.
- There's no color.
- It's "ugly."
- You can't sell flooring without mentioning specific products.
- It's "unprofessional."

According to conventional wisdom this seems like good sense. There's just one problem: The "experts" are dead wrong.

Steve D'Angelo is the owner of Main Place Floors in Cottonwood, Arizona. He sent this exact letter to a small, carefully targeted list and generated $29,073.79 in sales in a couple of weeks. This represented an 11-1 return on his marketing cost. One man purchased $14,337 worth of expensive tile, and he wasn't even on Steve's mailing list. The man's neighbor received the letter and gave it to him. "I've never seen a flooring ad compel this kind of response," Steve told me. "The majority of typical direct mail pieces sent out by flooring dealers get thrown in the trash with the rest of the junk mail without even being opened."

During the height of the Great Recession, Steve told me, "My sales have doubled and tripled." Using the Direct Response strategies in this book, Steve was able to survive and thrive during the recession while many of the other dealers in his area went out of business. He was almost literally the "last man standing," and was able to scoop up the market share left behind by his failed competitors.

And Steve is not the only one to achieve amazing success by breaking the rules. Many other dealers I coach have used the exact letter Steve used—or other letters just as long, ugly, and "unprofessional"—and have collectively generated millions of dollars.

And I practice what I preach. Letters like the one described here have been a part of my marketing mix for every business I've built, including *Flooring Success Systems*.

Using the strategies in this chapter and the next, you too can engineer Direct Response Marketing campaigns that give people an overwhelming reason to choose you instead of your competitors, and to refer others.

You've just got to be willing to break some rules.

Letters Vs. Brochures

Marketing letters are a great way to get very personal with your prospects and customers. They can be used in Tiers 1 and 2. For years I've been providing my *Flooring Success Systems* members with turn-key marketing letters like the one described above. They're cheaper to print than brochures, they're easy to create, they forge a strong connection with your customers, they look like a personal message you wrote and printed yourself, and they are easy to change if you decide to alter your marketing message. And most importantly, when done correctly these letters work. The hundreds of dealers I've coached have proven this.

This doesn't mean that brochures don't have their place. They do, as a sales tool *after* you have successfully gotten a customer into your store by using effective Direct Response Marketing.

Don't Be The Low Price Leader

"Live by price, die by price."

"If you aren't getting any price resistance, your prices are too low."

"Competing by low price requires the least talent and the least imagination."

"Low price is the default position of the lazy marketer."

Box stores exist by creating the perception of lowest price. This is their one selling point. They beat this mantra to death because they have nothing else to offer. Through loss leaders, category killers, and other techniques, they are masters at creating the *perception* of low price. However, in reality they are rarely a true low price leader. (A great book on this subject is *Walmart: The High Cost Of Low Prices* by Greg Spotts.)

Low price is a temporary market advantage at best

The problem is too many dealers try to copy the techniques employed by the box stores and create the perception that *they* are the low price leader. This is a suicide mission. If your market advantage is low price, you have nowhere to go but down. All it takes is for someone to come along and offer a lower price, and you've just lost your market advantage.

Problems with competing by low price

A lot of dealers believe that if they can attract more customers with a low price, they will make it up in volume. There are several *giant* problems with this.

1. You won't make it up in volume. Very few businesses can make up for low price with sales volume. Even the box stores succeed by creating the *perception* of low price. They really are not the lowest priced option. On top of that, they have the facilities to move gigantic amounts of merchandise (not flooring) in a short time. Selling and installing flooring is a long, complicated, labor-intensive process. You won't make it up in volume. And the math proves this. In his book *How To Sell At Prices Higher Than Your Competitors*, Dr. Larry Steinmetz reveals some math on price-cutting that is truly startling for most business owners. He shows that if you are selling on a 35% gross profit margin and you cut your prices by 10%, you have to *double* your gross sales to arrive at the same net profit. The lower your margins, the higher your gross sales need to be in order to compensate for a 10% price cut. (Conversely, if you *raise* your prices by 10%, you can lose up to 40% of your customers and still net the same amount.) Do you think that by cutting your prices by 10% you'll double your gross sales? Dream on. Something to think about if you're considering slashing your prices in order to "compete."

2. Your quality goes down the toilet. To make up for low price, you have to cram more sales into your month. This means everyone is rushed. There isn't time to provide good service because you're too busy trying to crank out the next sale, the next installation, etc.

Walmart is a shining example of what happens to customer service when you compete on cheap price. If I go to Walmart I expect only one thing: low price. I do not expect quality service. And it's a good thing, because I'd be disappointed most of the time. I can never find a salesperson when I need them, and when I do they never have the training to help me. The facilities are always dirty. The employees are disinterested. But I get my low price. (And I rarely go to Walmart.)

Think of any quality, successful business, whether it's a restaurant or a specialty shop, and the prices are always higher than the competitors'. Successful business owners know that quality and low price don't go together.

3. You have nowhere to go but down. If the only benefit you can offer to prospects is low price, what happens when someone comes along who is lower than you? You have no choice but to lower your price. Competing with low price is a dead-end street.

Raise Your Prices!

Here are some tips for raising your prices:

Build value in the minds of your prospects. If you build value into your service, you will be able to demand higher prices. If you build value in the minds of your prospects, most will gladly pay higher prices.

End comparison-shopping. If you are different from all the other stores, people are much more willing to pay a higher price. The idea is to get prospects to view your store as an orange, *the* orange, in a barrel full of apples. This is also accomplished through unique selling propositions, or USP's.

Serve prospects liberal quantities of adult beverages. (Kidding. Just making sure you're paying attention.)

Don't cater to "bottom-feeders." Some people are loyal to price. Whoever has the lowest price, that's who they are loyal to. You don't want these people. No matter how good your products are, or how much quality you build into your service, they still want the lowest price. Have you ever noticed that price shoppers are also the biggest complainers, nit-pickers, slow-pay-and-no-pay gigantic pains-in-the-ass? The minute you realize that you're dealing with a bottom feeder, send them to your competitor.

Educate your prospects. Educate prospects on the benefits of your dealership. Educate them on the difference between a quality dealership and buying from the cheap guys. Show them how you are different. *The Consumer's Guide To Floor Covering* that I told you about earlier is a sales letter, but it's also an education piece that dealers give to prospects. It creates total differentiation, positions the dealer as a trusted authority, educates prospects on how to choose a dealer, why cheap price and quality never go together, and helps the dealer command premium prices.

People accept the value *you* place on your services. People who are loyal to quality *expect* to pay a higher price, and are suspicious of low-priced services. I've lost track of how many times I've had customers tell me they got a flyer for a ridiculously low-priced service, but they didn't buy from that company because they were afraid of poor quality. That company may have done a good job, but they placed a low value on their services. This caused everyone else to place a low value on their service as well.

If you charge a high price for your products and services, people will generally accept that your price reflects your quality; that there is a good reason you are more expensive than others. In fact, if you are the most expensive dealership in your area, people will tend to view you as the highest quality.

I said earlier that I used to own a carpet cleaning company. Cleaning carpets basically boils down to removing dirt from fabric. Talk about boring. Talk about commoditized. Talk about difficult to create differentiation. Yet I made sure we were the highest priced in town. If I found out another carpet cleaner had higher prices, I'd raise mine again. I did this in part because I knew that people would accept the value I placed on my service, and I wanted my company to be seen as being the best.

You have nowhere to go but up. Once you have established yourself as the quality leader (not the low-price leader), you will attract customers who are interested in quality, and who don't mind paying more. You will never be put into a position of having to beat another store's prices. This makes it much easier to raise prices when necessary. Customers who buy from you and refer people to you do so because they want the best. Price increases are not a big deal. Not so with stores that compete on low price.

If the only thing people were interested in was low price, everyone would eat at McDonald's. Yet we know that people go to extremely expensive restaurants and gladly pay the exorbitant prices. And leave a big tip! They are judging the restaurant on something other than price. Service, atmosphere, and quality of food.

Make no mistake, there are many reasons people choose stores other than price. Just educate them on all the reasons they should choose you instead of all the other cheap guys.

Watch Out!

Avoid This Shortcut To Bankruptcy

In his book *How To Sell At Prices Higher Than Your Competitors*, Dr. Larry Steinmetz says that most businesses that go bankrupt do so during a period of increasing sales and decreasing margins.

Translation: They bite the dust selling a lot of stuff on the cheap.

Don't kid yourself: Selling on cheap price will catch up with you. Maybe you won't go bankrupt, but you'll likely always struggle, and have to endure the endless stress and frustration of having to "beat" the other guy's price.

Understanding Front End Vs. Back End

Front end is what you make on the initial sale to a customer. Back end is what you make from repeat and referral sales over the course of your relationship with that customer. The cost of gaining a new customer is so expensive that 5/45 dealers don't ignore back end. They know this is where the lion's share of the profits is made. In some industries, the business actually loses money to gain a new customer. All their money is made from back end.

Lifetime Value of a Customer

As I demonstrated earlier, every prospect that walks through your door is worth anywhere from $25,000 to $80,000 or more. But most floor dealers and their sales teams are transaction oriented, only considering the value of the sale right in front of them, with little or no thought given to the Lifetime Value of a Customer (LVC).

Using Message, Market, and Media

How many times have you had this happen: The ad salesman for your local paper catches you as you're headed to lunch to let you know they're having a "this-week-only-half-off" special on full-page ads, but they need your submission in the next 24 hours? Or the guy who sells imprinted promotional items wanders into your office to sell you personalized pens, magnets, golf tees, gym bags, water bottles, live puppies, and anything else they can stick a logo on?

Unfortunately, many flooring dealers will jump at these kinds of spur-of-the-moment "opportunities." This is *advertising by the seat of your pants*, and it almost always results in marketing decisions that make a lot of money ... for the guy selling the ad. Not for the floor dealer. The financial returns for dealers who use seat-of-the-pants advertising are inconsistent at best; disastrous at worst.

Dealers allow themselves to be lured into these kinds of poor advertising decisions because they have no marketing plan in place. No goal, no system, no true objective other than some vague notion of "getting their name out there." So they stumble from one advertising media to another, never really sure what's working and what's not, and never really in control of their marketing. Well in today's incredibly competitive market this is simply not good enough, especially for the small business owner who cannot afford waste and has to make every advertising dollar count.

One of the best ways to regain control of your marketing is by using the 3-Tier system I discussed earlier.

Another valuable tool is the concept of Message, Market, and Media, which I learned from Dan Kennedy. I've used this for nearly 20 years as a guide when assembling marketing campaigns. It works like this:

Message

This is what you have to say in your marketing about your dealership to your ideal prospect. This is where you educate your prospects about the tremendous benefits of using your services, make an irresistible offer, and otherwise give them the information they need to choose *you* instead of your competitors.

Market

These are your ideal prospects; the kinds of people who are predisposed to buy from you. They want your products, are willing to pay your prices, will use you again, and will refer others. Choosing the correct market is critical. Even if you have a fantastic message delivered with the perfect media, you can still fail if you don't choose your market correctly. A mediocre message delivered to the right market is far better than a great message delivered to the wrong market.

Dealers often ask me, "What demographic should I market to?" or "Should I buy a list of prospects?" I always reply by asking if they are marketing to the most valuable and responsive list of proven buyers of flooring available: *their past customers*. Most aren't (insanity!), so my recommendation is to begin there. Once they're marketing to their past customers with a monthly newsletter, then they can move on to other demographics. Which demographics? It depends upon a lot of factors. But a good shortcut is to analyze your current customer list—proven buyers of your product—and market to others who share characteristics with those on your list. This could mean those who live in certain neighborhoods or certain kinds of neighborhoods, income levels, professions, etc.

Media

This is how the message is delivered to your prospects. Every medium has different levels of effectiveness, cost variances, and different limitations. Here is a partial list of media:

- Website
- Direct mail
- SEO
- Social media
- Display ads

- Postcards

- Valpak

- Signage

- Newspaper

- Internet

- Radio

- Television

- Billboards

Message, market, and media are all used in every campaign. The question is whether you'll use them effectively or ineffectively. They are like a three-legged stool: If one leg is weak the stool will collapse. They are equally important, and you can begin with any of the three. For example, your message one month might be a special offer for a free extended warranty on a particular brand of carpet. Your market is households that have two or more children under the age of 18. Since the market you are trying to reach is very specific, the media you choose is direct mail so you can pinpoint exactly who gets your message.

By approaching every advertising campaign in terms of message, market, and media—and always using the 3-Tier approach—you will regain control of your marketing and stop being an advertising victim.

Sales And Marketing Systems

Each strategy I talk about in this book will work individually; you can approach them "cafeteria" style. However, they are designed to work together as a system. Each strategy draws power from the other strategies. They complement each other. The more strategies you implement into your sales and marketing, the stronger each *individual* strategy becomes. Your efforts are compounded. Think of 10 pieces of string. They each might be capable of supporting one pound of weight, 10 pounds total. However, if you braid the individual pieces into a single rope, they will be able to support 100 pounds. By working together, their strength is increased exponentially. It's the same with these strategies. The more you implement, the more effective each individual strategy becomes, and the more powerful your marketing machine will become.

"What Kind Of Advertising Should I Do First?"

A dealer asked me this during a private coaching session. It's a question I get asked a lot, and no wonder. There are hundreds of ways to promote your flooring business, both online and offline, and some of them require a substantial investment. (Especially if they involve giving away free beer.)

To make matters worse, every print ad rep, promotional gift item rep, web designer, radio and TV advertising rep, and SEO "expert" who mails, calls, or bumbles into your store claims that you should start with whatever *they* happen to be selling. Many dealers wind up buying whatever gets suggested to them, in other words, marketing by the seat of their pants.

It's easy to get overwhelmed by all the options and contradictory advice.

The solution is to use the Three Tiers of Marketing I discussed earlier. This approach will revolutionize your business, and give you a huge competitive advantage over all the other dealers in your area. I recommend going back and reading that chapter.

Unique Selling Proposition

I'll explain what a unique selling proposition is by first telling you what it is *not*. It is not a *universal* selling proposition. A universal selling proposition is something that everyone in a certain business category has. Almost all doctors offer free consultations. That's a universal selling proposition. The same with free estimates from floor dealers.

A unique selling proposition, on the other hand, is something that is unique to your business. It's something that almost no one in your business category offers. It separates you from everyone else. Here are two powerful examples:

- When it absolutely, positively has to be there overnight (FedEx)
- Fresh, hot pizza delivered in 30 minutes or less (Domino's Pizza)

Both of these companies built business empires on the strength of their respective USP's.

A good USP is not general, it's specific; it focuses like a laser beam on a specific, obvious benefit to the prospect. The benefit promised by FedEx is clear and unambiguous. The same with Domino's.

Most dealers try to be all things to all people, and consequently they wind up using generic descriptions of their business. Look at any floor covering ad and you will likely see one of the following adjectives or phrases: *Trusted, Friendly, Professional, Free Quotes, Best Value, 100% Satisfaction*. These mean absolutely nothing to the consumer because they convey no clear, compelling benefit. They also have zero impact because *everybody* says it!

Compare the examples above with FedEx's unique selling proposition: *When it absolutely, positively has to be there overnight.* This gives a specific, clear, easily understood benefit to the customer. It focuses like a laser beam, and gives the customer an obvious reason to use FedEx instead of all the other mailing services. Ask yourself this question: *Why should my prospect choose my business versus any/every other floor dealer available to them?* By coming up with a clear, compelling answer to that question, you'll have your USP.

USP's are so critical to a floor dealer's success that I've developed turnkey USP's that my *Flooring Success Systems* members use to promote their flooring businesses. These USP's create total differentiation between my members' businesses and their competitors, and help them to command premium prices in any market.

Guarantees As USP

People are skeptical, and for good reason. At one time or another almost everyone has been ripped off, cheated, or been disappointed by inferior quality. A guarantee will go a long way toward soothing your prospect's fears about buying from you. Shout your guarantees and warranties from the mountaintops, let everyone know, put them in all your marketing material. People will think, "Wow, if this guy is so sure about his store that he keeps offering these guarantees, it must be pretty good!"

Powerful guarantees and warranties will go a long way in establishing solid credibility with skeptical customers, and toward easing their fears. Unless you use a lot of "weasel" clauses. You know, the fine print. What the guarantee giveth, the fine print taketh away, and your prospects know this. If you have a great guarantee but you include 16 pages of fine print giving you all kinds of "outs," you are defeating one of the major benefits of a strong guarantee: risk reversal.

Risk Reversal

Effective guarantees and warranties can function as risk reversal for your prospects. For example, flooring prospects are afraid of investing thousands of dollars in flooring, and then not liking it after it's been installed. To counter this, a lot of the co-ops have a replacement guarantee that's good for 30-60 days after the purchase. The customer can get the flooring replaced one time at no cost, and the co-op picks up the tab for the dealer. This reverses the risk of making a flooring purchase the prospect will regret.

Here are some key areas that prospects feel place them at risk when buying flooring: 1) regretting their purchase; 2) scary-looking/ unprofessional installers; 3) problems with the installation itself; 4) late or missed appointments; and 5) phone calls not returned. How many others can you think of? Your job is to create compelling guarantees that overcome these fears.

Borrow From Other Industries

If you don't borrow from outside your industry, you are doomed to copy those within it. You can certainly see this in the flooring industry.

Walk into 10 flooring stores at random and you'll hear the same opening line from virtually every salesperson: "How may I help you?" or "What kind of flooring did you have in mind?" (Earlier you learned why using these openers virtually guarantees that you'll get beat up on price.)

Virtually all flooring retail websites use the *Name, Rank, and Serial Number* formula.

Showrooms look basically the same from one dealer to the next. Yes, some do a better job of making their showrooms more elegant, but very few create true differentiation.

Bottom line: Most flooring dealerships look, feel, smell, and act exactly like one another; any differences tend to be cosmetic. In their visuals, marketing, sales processes, and actions, very few dealers answer the unspoken question on every prospect's mind: *Why should I do business with you versus every other option available to me, including doing nothing?*

One way to counter this is to look outside the flooring industry for sales and marketing inspiration. Some of the biggest breakthroughs in business have come when one industry borrows from another. Banks borrowed the drive-through concept from the fast food industry. It's now been adopted by dry cleaners, pharmacies, even Vegas wedding chapels!

Case in point: As discussed earlier, I train floor dealers to use my trademarked sales process called the *Design Audit*™. The *Design Audit*™ does several critical jobs for dealers and their sales teams:

- Creates total differentiation from other dealers
- Positions the dealer/sales team as Trusted Advisors (rather than "salesmen" hocking flooring)
- Reduces/eliminates price resistance
- Creates upsell opportunities that don't *feel* like upsells
- Dramatically increases dealers' closed-sale batting average

Many parts of the *Design Audit*™ I borrowed from the medical industry, the food industry, carpet cleaning, and others. By borrowing from outside the flooring industry I was able to create a tool for dealers that has enabled big breakthroughs in their businesses, especially in being able to sell at premium prices.

....

THIRTEEN

HOW TO CREATE KILLER ADS

FLOOR DEALER: What do you think of my display ad?

JIM: It has your business name at the top, photos of products, and contact information.

FLOOR DEALER: Right. It's full color, very professional.

JIM: But does it answer the unspoken question on your prospects' minds: Why should I do business with you instead of your competitors?

FLOOR DEALER: Well ...

The Cardinal Sin of Marketing

Recently I was having a terrible time falling asleep, and after a week of insomnia I went bleary-eyed to my doctor to get help.

"Doctor, I've tried sleeping pills, reading, watching The Weather Channel, counting rolls of carpet, but nothing works," I told him, desperation in my voice. "I've barely slept in seven days. Can you help me?"

He stroked his chin and gazed out the window, as if struggling to make a decision. Finally he said, "I can prescribe a treatment that will virtually guarantee that you will fall asleep. But," he held up a cautionary finger, "I only use it in extreme cases, and I must warn you to be very careful. Do not drive while using this treatment. And make sure you are lying down because it works almost instantly."

"I'll try anything, Doc. What is it?"

He opened a drawer, removed a manila envelope and handed it to me. "Remember, be careful."

I opened the envelope and began pulling out pieces of paper that turned out to be advertisements for flooring. As I thumbed through the ads I felt my eyes grow heavy. My head swam; suddenly everything went dark.

The sharp odor of smelling salts jolted me awake, and next thing I knew the doctor was helping me off the floor.

"What happened?" I asked.

"You fell asleep," he replied. "A long time ago I discovered that most flooring advertisements are an excellent cure for insomnia."

"Why?" I asked.

"Because they're so boring," he replied. "They can make a ride in a golf cart seem like a triple-loop roller coaster by comparison."

"Oh thank you, doctor," I said, throwing my arms around him, tears of gratitude filling my eyes. "Thank you, thank you!"

What a relief to have a guaranteed cure for my insomnia! However, because my business is helping floor dealers increase the size of their bank accounts through effective marketing, I couldn't help but be alarmed that so many dealers are throwing away their money on ads and websites that put their prospects to sleep. I knew it was my duty to take action, which is why I wrote this book.

The cardinal sin of advertising is being boring. If your ads are boring, then they won't hold your prospect's attention and compel them to take the desired action. Here are some common ways that dealers bore prospects with their ads and websites:

- Using ads and websites that look the same as everyone else's. Most dealers use the aforementioned *Name, Rank, and Serial Number* formula. These ads and websites may have cosmetic differences (different colors, different graphics, etc.) but they mostly *say* the same thing and mostly *look* the same. (Boring.)

- They don't answer the unspoken question on every prospect's mind: *"Why should I buy from you instead of your competitor?"* (Including the dealer down the street, box stores, online discount dealers, as well as buying from no one at all.)

- They contain no unique selling proposition. Instead, they mostly contain slogans that are meaningless to the prospect, such as "Number One In Customer Satisfaction," or "Serving the Tri-State Area For 267 Years," or "We'll Floor You With Our Service." (Zzzzzz.)

- They don't educate the prospect. They don't provide information on how to choose a flooring dealer; tough questions to ask a dealer before buying anything; common misconceptions about flooring; why cheap price and quality don't go together; the dangers of buying from box stores or online discounters, etc.

- The offers are weak, copycat, "me-too" offers. You seldom see anything the prospect would find compelling, interesting, fun, different, or engaging.

Here's an exercise: Pull up your website and any ads you've run in the past six months. Using the list above as a gauge, would a prospect find your advertising compelling or boring? Be honest; it's *your* business and *your* ad dollars at stake. If your advertising is on the boring end of the spectrum—and you are courageous enough to admit it—then you can take meaningful action to correct this problem.

Marketing Principles Are Universal

The Direct Response Marketing principles in this chapter, and throughout this book, work in any media: websites, mobile marketing, social media, print, direct mail, letters, postcards, email, door hangers, signage, etc. Keep this in mind if I give an example using a postcard or a letter. Don't make the mistake of thinking that just because you are using a website that the rules of Direct Response no longer apply. They do.

 ## "Ugly" Outperforms Pretty

Studies have shown that ugly ads outperform pretty ads, lots of copy outperforms white space, cluttered outperforms non-cluttered. My own experience, and that of hundreds of dealers I've coached, has verified this. Remember what I said earlier: People are bombarded with thousands of advertising messages a day. No one can possibly absorb this much information, so people put up advertising filters. You do it, I do it, and your prospects and customers do it. Your job as a marketer is to cut through their filter, grab their attention, and compel them to respond.

Remember the ugly, cardboard garage sale sign I mentioned earlier? After driving through town with my advertising filter on full blast and not even noticing the dozens of fancy, flashing, expensive business signs, that cardboard sign did what all the others couldn't: It got my attention.

I'm not saying you should advertise by scrawling your message on a piece of cardboard. I told you about that cardboard sign because I want you to shift your thinking about marketing and advertising. It's not about you, your image, your logo, or your ego. It's 100% about maximizing sales, even if it means using advertising some "experts" would consider "ugly."

Secrets To Writing Copy That Sells

Forget what your English teacher taught you

Some people think they can never learn to write good copy because they are "no good" at English and grammar and punctuation. Well, let me tell you, the best copy breaks all the rules of grammar. Some of my most profitable sales letters would give an English teacher a raging fit. So don't get hung up about punctuation and good grammar.

Write like you talk.

Write your letters and ads just like you are talking to a prospect. After all, your letters, ads, and websites are your salesmen. They are literally "talking" for you. So make them sound like you are talking face to face with a prospect. Use sentence fragments. Use one-word sentences. Seriously. Again, don't stress about grammar and punctuation. The only "grade" that counts in copywriting is how much money the ad puts into your bank account.

Talk from the heart

Pour your heart into your copy. If you really believe in your service (and you should), express how you feel. One way to do this is to start with a rough draft. When you write your rough draft, just let the words pour out. Don't worry about formatting, punctuation, spelling … nothing except getting the words onto paper. You can tidy it up later. Right now you are trying to capture pure emotion. Just talk from the heart, keep it simple, and talk about the benefits to your customers. After you do this, go back and do your editing for your final product.

Create an attention-grabbing headline

Your headline is the most important part of the letter. It's the "ad for the ad." It's what creates the initial interest that gets people to stop and read your letter. A good way to come up with a great headline is to sit in a quiet place for about 30 minutes and write every possible headline that comes into your mind. Don't worry about how weird or unusable some of them might seem. Just write them down. You should be able to come up with 20-30 headlines. Pick the best one. The five or six runner-up headlines become your subheadings throughout the letter. (Extensive market testing has shown that while using the headline "Buy Flooring From Me And I Won't Kidnap Your Dog" is attention-grabbing, and it *does* contain a benefit, it will not result in increased sales. Increased visits from police officers, yes. Increased sales, no.)

Use attention grabbing subheads

The subheadings keep the reader interested. They are "mini-ads" for the upcoming paragraph.

Subheads also create a double-readership path. Some people will read every single word of your letter; these are your detailed readers. Some will merely scan the letter; these are your "skimmers." The subheads ensure that skimmers get your marketing message even though they don't read all the details. Two readership paths: one for the detailed readers, one for the skimmers.

Get the reader to turn the page

When using letters, I try to end each page with an incomplete sentence, with the remainder of the sentence coming on the following page. This is done on purpose to get the reader to turn the page. Other devices can be used to accomplish this:

Ask a question at the bottom of the page, and then answer it on the next page.

Create curiosity. End the page with a phrase like, "Turn the page to find out how to get a free gift worth $197!"

Have a message that says "Turn To Next Page" or "OVER."

Always use a postscript

Some readers will simply skip to the end of the letter. That's why the postscript or P.S. is so important. Use the P.S. to restate your offer, deadline, one or two key benefits, and call to action. The idea is to sum up the most important points in the letter.

Don't be boring

Remember that the only thing people care about is benefits to them. Every point and every feature of your letter should be framed in terms of benefits to the reader.

Use Secondary Response Mechanisms

Most dealers' ads, letters, postcards, and websites have only two ways for the prospect to respond: call or visit the flooring store.

Many people are intimidated by calling or visiting because they are afraid they'll have to talk to a pushy salesperson, or that they'll get ripped off. Secondary response mechanisms give the prospect other ways to get information before contacting you directly. Think of a secondary response mechanism as going on a date before asking the person to marry you.

Some examples of good secondary response mechanisms include:

- Your web address

- An offer for a free report or consumer guide

- A free recorded message (This can be a recorded version of the free report. Provide prospects access on your website, and/or by calling a free recorded message hotline.)

- Testimonial hotline (Prospects call a toll-free number or visit the testimonial page on your website and hear recorded testimonials from your happy customers.)

Features Vs. Benefits

"Everybody's favorite radio station is W.I.I.F.M. — 'What's In It For Me?'"

Look at floor dealer ads or websites and you will see virtually every business listing their features. Things like:

- Family owned and operated
- Professional installers
- Lifetime warranty
- Lists of products

This all sounds very nice and professional. There's only one teensy, tiny, little problem: *Nobody cares about features!* Listing features has little to no impact in the mind of your potential customer. The only thing your prospects care about (and I mean the only thing) is *benefits*.

Prospects don't care about professional installers. That is, they won't care unless you educate them about how they will benefit from having a professional installer. By listing the benefits of using professional installers, prospects will now truly appreciate the fact that you employ them to install your products. "Professional installers" is no longer just a feature; it's a benefit that adds value to your service.

This is how you should approach every single feature of your dealership. Because we work in the flooring industry, you and I know the value of certain flooring-related features, but don't assume that your prospects know. Assume that they know nothing. Learn to think in terms of benefits to your prospect whenever you put together a marketing campaign.

How Long Should My Ad Or Sales Letter Be?

Long enough to tell your entire marketing story. Remember, a person who is not interested in flooring won't read 10 words, but someone who is interested will read 10 pages.

Many of the ads and letters in my *Flooring Success Systems* program are two or more pages long. People tell me all the time, "No one will read a long sales letter." Most ad agencies and ad salesmen will tell you to use as few words as possible. They want you to buy the biggest ad you can possibly afford, use a lot of color, put your logo at the top, and leave a lot of empty space. These ads look extremely slick and professional; they just don't work very well for dealers.

Remember: The more you tell, the more you sell.

Watch Out!  Don't Listen To Your Printer

When you begin switching to Direct Response Marketing, you may get unsolicited advice from your printer, ad rep, webmaster, brother-in-law, etc., because the ads don't follow the Name, Rank, and Serial Number formula everyone is used to seeing. They may suggest that your webpages, ads, letters, etc., are too "wordy," that your copy is too long, or that you need more "white space." They may show you other flooring ads as examples of what you should do.

If I had listened to the advice given to me by printers, ad reps, and web designers, I'd be getting the same lousy results most floor dealers get with their ads. And I'd probably be broke, out of business, or both!

These people may mean well, but they are not marketing experts. Follow their advice at your own peril.

Proven Formulas For Direct Response Ads, Letters, and Websites

There are a lot of good Direct Response formulas, but it's beyond the scope of this book to explore them all. For now I'm going to give you two of the most effective, time-tested-and-proven formulas. My dealers and I have used these formulas to collectively generate millions of dollars.

A.I.D.A. Formula (Attention, Interest, Desire, Action)

Attention—Get your prospect's attention with a captivating headline. The headline is the "ad for the ad." The headline makes people want to read your ad, letter, or website.

Interest—Create interest for your prospect with a strong first paragraph. The first paragraph, or section, of your ad or letter should feature the most powerful benefits. Keep the interest of your reader throughout the letter with subheadings. Also, don't be boring!

Desire—Create desire in your prospect with the "irresistible offer."

Action—Give your prospect a call to action at the end of the ad or letter. Tell them to *"call right now!"* Always use a deadline. A Direct Response piece is not Direct Response without a deadline.

P.A.S. Formula (Problem, Agitate, Solve)

Problem—Inform your prospect that they have a problem or a potential problem.

Agitate—Go into great detail about the problem. This is where you "rub salt in the wound."

Solve—Give your prospect the solution to the problem. Obviously the solution is going to be you.

A twist on this is:

Problem

Agitate

Invalidate (all other solutions besides the one you are offering)

Solve

Make Sure Your Letters Get Opened

How many times have you pulled a big stack of mail out of your mailbox and stood next to the trash can, putting your bills and letters in one pile, but throwing anything that even LOOKS like junk mail into the trash without opening it? Well, make no mistake: If you're doing direct mail, your potential customers are doing the exact same thing with *your* mailers. And if your ads are getting thrown away unopened, well, my friend ... you're out of the game before it even starts.

The TRUTH is there is *enormous* waste in the vast majority of direct mail campaigns. Studies show that on average 60% of direct mail gets thrown out *unopened*! Because of this, big corporations do direct mail campaigns with response rates that are tiny fractions of 1%. As a small business owner, you cannot afford this waste. Yet when most dealers do a direct mail campaign they try to copy the "big boys," and wind up flushing a ton of money down the toilet.

I teach over a dozen strategies that virtually guarantee your direct mail gets opened and your message seen. Here's one that you can put to use immediately:

Strategy #6 out of 17 for getting your mailers opened: Three-Dimensional Mail

Imagine you're sorting your mail over the trash, tossing out the junk mail, when you come across an envelope that has something thick and lumpy in it. Are you going to toss it out without at least finding out what's inside? Most likely not. Well, your prospects are unlikely to throw it out without at least opening it either.

What should you put in the envelope to make it lumpy? All kinds of things. For example, my members use a "Lifesaver Letter," which is mailed out with a pack of Life Savers candies inside. The headline of the letter says, "Do You Need A 'Lifesaver' To Help You Navigate The Turbulent Waters Of Buying New Floors?" Another letter contains a small rubber brain. The headline says, "Here's An Offer That's A No-Brainer!"

My dealers and I have used dice, toy bugs, packets of aspirin, and other items with fantastic success. My "Shock-And-Awe" campaign uses a series of dimensional mailers sent to prospects who have visited the dealer's store, but didn't make a purchase. It's designed to stop the "shopping" in its tracks, create total differentiation from other dealers, remind the prospect of the unique benefits of buying from that dealer, and compel them to return to the store and make a purchase. This campaign has had phenomenal success in large part because of the dimensional aspect. One of my dealers used this campaign to land a $20,000 commercial flooring job even though he was the highest bidder.

One reason (among several) for the success of these mailers is that they get a virtual 100% open rate because people's curiosity always gets the best of them. Also, it's difficult to stack other letters on top of lumpy mailers, so they get put on top of the pile.

Dealers have reported tremendous response and great feedback from people receiving these mailers. They give your prospects a smile and brighten their day. It creates an instant connection with the prospect and makes the dealer seem like a real, live person with a sense of humor. (Remember, people want to do business with people, not impersonal corporations.)

Two important points about dimensional mailers: 1) You must tie in your marketing message to the object in the letter; and 2) these cost more to send out than regular mailers, so you want to use a highly targeted list.

Amazing Waste

One day I was speaking to a flooring dealer in Florida. I asked him how much he was spending on his advertising.

"$20,000 per month," he replied.

"What kind of results are you getting?" I asked.

"Lousy."

$20,000 a month. Lousy results. Ouch. Yet this fellow was unwilling to learn new methods for marketing his business. Double ouch.

I've found this to be a common phenomenon. Some dealers are so resistant to change that they'd rather flush thousands of dollars per month down the toilet on lousy advertising, or miss out on thousands of dollars in additional sales they could get if they were open to learning effective marketing techniques. For some dealers, failure is preferable to change.

One-Step And Two-Step Marketing

There are two main methods for using marketing to generate sales.

- One-step marketing (also called "immediate sale")
- Two-step marketing (also called "lead generation")

One-step marketing

With one-step marketing you put out an ad, letter, postcard, email, or other media that has a direct offer to buy. In other words, it goes for the immediate sale. For example, you run an ad that offers a discount or a free gift if they purchase within a specified time. You are trying to get prospects to immediately visit your store or call you based solely on the strength of this letter. Done correctly, this is an extremely effective method for generating sales, and there are endless ways to do it.

Two-step marketing

This is also called "lead generation." With two-step marketing, you are *not* trying to get an immediate sale. You are trying to build a very hot list of interested prospects. You then do follow-up marketing to these prospects.

My dealers have access to a done-for-them free report called *The Consumer's Guide To Floor Covering*. Visitors to these dealers' websites see a message that says:

WARNING! Don't call or visit any floor dealer until you read this free consumer's guide. You will discover how to avoid predatory dealers, 6 mistakes to avoid when choosing a flooring store, 3 dirty little secrets about installation that some dealers pray you never find out, and 5 questions to ask a dealer before you buy.

In order to get the report, prospects have to provide their contact information. This is called "opting in." Once they've opted in, the prospect gets the free report, and the dealer is able to do follow-up marketing. As they collect these names and addresses, dealers are building a hot, customized list of prospects who have shown a high level of interest in flooring. By marketing to this list they get a much higher response than from a purchased list. Why? Because out of the general population of their market area—which could be hundreds-of-thousands of people—these people have raised their hands and said, "I'm interested." You can also spend more on marketing to these hot prospects, like using dimensional mailers.

Two-step marketing is an extremely effective way to generate sales. However, the vast majority of dealers, including box stores, are either unaware of this marketing method, or they don't know how to do it, or they're too lazy to do it, so it's rarely used. This gives dealers who know how to do two-step marketing another advantage over their competitors.

Sequential Marketing

Have you ever been late paying a bill, or known someone who was late? First you receive a letter from the company politely asking you to give them money to pay off your bill. Then a week or two later you receive a letter marked "2nd Notice" that refers to the first notice and has a more strongly worded message to please give them money. A week or two later you receive a letter marked "3rd Notice" that refers to the previous two letters and has an even more strongly worded message to please give them money. Now. Or dire consequences will result. (Like getting a late-night visit from two large fellows named "Lefty" and "Knuckles" to explain their incentive plan for prompt payment.)

Let's think about this. Collection companies have been using this technique successfully for decades to pry money out of the hands of people who *don't* have any money, who *hate* them, and who will receive *nothing* in return once payment is made. If a collection company can get money from people under these extremely adverse conditions, why can't a business owner use the same technique on people who DON'T hate them, who HAVE money to spend, and will RECEIVE something they want in exchange for their money?

That's where sequential marketing comes in. Sequential marketing can be done with letters, postcards, email, fax, flyers, etc., or a combination of media.

Here's an example using a three-letter sequence: Send out letter #1 featuring an offer with a deadline 30 days in the future. Two weeks later, send letter #2 to everyone who didn't respond to letter #1. The second letter should reference the first letter, and repeat the offer and the deadline. Two weeks later, send letter #3 to everyone who didn't respond to the first two letters. Letter #3 references the first two letters, and repeats the offer and the deadline. Each letter has an escalating sense of urgency about it.

There are endless ways you can use multiple media. For example, in between letters you can also send postcards, emails, flyers, etc., to create excitement and further heighten the sense of urgency in your prospect. The mix you use will vary depending upon your list, your budget, the offer, etc.

Another reason sequential mailings are so powerful is because most of your prospects are leading busy, hectic lives. Example: Ron and Mary Jones have three kids ranging from fifth through tenth grade who are all involved in sports, music, martial arts, etc. Ron commutes to work and is gone 50+ hours per week, and Mary volunteers at her church and at the local Red Cross. Ron and Mary are busy and frazzled. She gets your first letter and thinks, "Hey, this sounds really good. And Ron and I have been talking about getting new carpet soon." So she sets your letter aside intending to get to it later. Then she gets a call from the Red Cross and they need some last minute help on a project. At the same time, the teacher for her fifth-grader calls and wants to meet to discuss homework that's not being completed. The letter gets forgotten and as the days pass it gets buried under other paperwork that Mary intends to "get to." But a week or two later Mary gets another letter from you, referencing the first letter, and restating the offer and deadline. And a week or two after that she gets a third letter.

If you sent her only one letter—like most businesses do—there's a good chance that you'd lose this sale. However, by sending sequential mailings you have cut through the clutter of Mary's busy life, reminded her of your message, and heightened the sense of urgency. This is another strategy that my dealers and I have used to generate tons of money.

Jim's Quick Checklist Of Direct Response Marketing Elements

1. **Headline**—Attention-grabbing, benefit-laden headline. (Tip: Business names are rarely a benefit; therefore, they almost always make lousy headlines. Here's an exception: *Same Day Flowers* is an example of a business name that conveys a benefit.)

2. **Subheads**—Creates a double-readership path. Some people are readers, some are skimmers. Subheads give skimmers all the key benefits.

3. **Why should your prospect believe you**—Anything to build credibility. Experience, certifications, etc. Explain WHY certifications, experience, etc., are of benefit.

4. **Big promise**—"Your friends will be dazzled by your luxurious Karastan area rug displayed over your brand new hardwood floors!" "Once they see your new floors, your friends will think you remodeled your entire home!"

5. **Testimonials**—What others say about you is 100 times more powerful than what you say about yourself, even if you're 100 times more eloquent.

6. **Who you are**—The copy should be very personal. They should see that you are a real, live, flesh-and-blood human being. Don't use "advertise-ese." (*We at Boring Flooring strive to be number one in customer satisfaction, provide superior service, and blah, blah, blah.* That's advertise-ese.)

7. **Drama**—Show before and after photos of your work. Photos of happy customers.

8. **Guarantees**—Use big, bold guarantees to separate you from everyone else, and remove any "risk" the prospects may perceive.

9. **Offer**—"Visit our showroom" is not an offer. "Call or visit now to get every 4th room free" is an offer. Tell them exactly what to do and exactly what they'll get for doing it.

10. **Deadline/call to action**—"You must call or visit by Friday, June 22nd, to get the special." Be very specific with your deadline. Usually if there is no deadline, your offer is not complete.

11. **P.S.**—Restate the offer, deadline, one or two key benefits, or a point that needs emphasis.

12. **Secondary response mechanism**—Include your main phone number and address, but also include your website, a free recorded message, or an offer for a free report or consumer guide.

Not every ad will have room for every element. I consider the top three elements to be: 1) Headline; 2) Testimonials; and 3) Offer with deadline.

I'll add other elements as space permits and as the situation warrants. One advantage of letters is that there are no space limitations. You can make the letter as long as you need it to be. In display ads, postcards, etc., you are limited. This does not make them bad media, but it does mean you have to give careful thought as to which elements to include. A small display ad will sometimes take as long to create as a multi-page letter because I have to be a lot choosier about what I include in the ad. With a letter, I can throw in everything *plus* the kitchen sink!

More ad writing tips ...

Get the headline right—I usually sit in a quiet place and force myself to write a couple of dozen headlines. Open your mind up and think of every possible benefit, or compelling idea, no matter how trivial or silly it seems at the time. The headline is the ad for the ad. Your business name does not make a good headline because your business name doesn't convey a benefit to the prospect, especially if they've never heard of you. People who don't already know you, like you, or trust you don't care about your business name because there's no relationship (sorry). There are only three things your prospects and customers care about: benefits, benefits, benefits. (You'll notice that "business name" isn't one of the three.) Yet the vast majority of flooring ads have the business name at the top. Big mistake.

What brilliant marketers have to say about headlines:

David Ogilvy, one of the brightest marketing minds ever, says: "On the average, five times as many people read the headlines as read the body copy. It follows that unless your headline sells your product, you have wasted 90% of your money."

Victor Schwab, author of *How To Write A Good Advertisement*, says: "Some of the most tremendous flops among advertisements contain body matter filled with convincing copy. But it just wasn't encapsulated into a good headline. And so the excellent copy didn't even get a reading."

Ted Nicholas, master of Direct Response Marketing, says: "... I spend hours on headlines—days if necessary. And when I get a good headline, I know that my task is nearly finished. Writing the copy can usually be done in a short time, if necessary. And that advertisement will be a good one—that is, if the headline is really a 'stopper.'"

Prioritize the benefits—The strongest benefit first. In fact, the strongest benefit often becomes my headline. The runner-ups become my subheads.

Powerful words to use in headlines—FREE, You, Yours, You Get, Amazing, Proven, Powerful, How To, Bonus, Money, Results, Discover, Health, Proven, Easy, New, Love, Safety, Save, Secret.

Tips on creating subheads—Remember that subheads create a double-readership path. Some people will read every single word, others will skim. The subhead creates a readership path for the skimmers. I've written out subheads on 3x5 cards, spread them out on a table, and then arranged them into a logical, story-telling sequence. This creates the outline for my entire online sales page, ad, or letter.

Deliver on the ad's promise—The headline should connect immediately with the copy in the online sales page or ad. If the headline creates anxiety, your first paragraph should address/exacerbate the anxiety. If the headline describes a benefit, get to the benefit right away.

Turn features into benefits—"Certified Installers" is a feature. Explain exactly how and why the customer will benefit from "Certified Installers." Never forget that everyone's favorite radio station is W.I.I.F.M.—What's In it For Me? There are only three things people care about: benefits, benefits, benefits.

Ask for the sale—Close the damn sale! After all, that's why you're investing the money in marketing! Give them a very concrete call to action with a deadline.

Don't forget the ultimate reason for the ad—The ultimate reason is not to be cute, funny, get your name out there, promote your logo, or stroke your ego. The ultimate purpose is to compel the prospect to call or visit your store and buy from you right away!

....

FOURTEEN

HOW TO GET BUSINESSES TO SEND YOU REFERRALS FOR FREE

FLOOR DEALER: We have three Realtors and a designer who send us referrals.

JIM: How much revenue per year?

FLOOR DEALER: About $100,000.

JIM: Imagine if you had 30 Realtors and designers sending you referrals.

Oil Cans Vs. Oil Wells

Most dealers spend their time, energy, and money trying to acquire oil cans (single transactions). You should think in terms of building oil wells. When you obtain a can of oil, your very next job is to go out and find another can of oil. Then another, and another, and so on. However, when you dig an oil well, you do the work one time and it produces oil forever. Your job is simply to maintain the oil well. Affiliate relationships with other businesses are oil wells.

I and the dealers I coach have made a truckload of money through affiliate relationships. The most powerful thing about affiliate relationships is that you do the work of setting them up *one time*, and then you reap the profits for years to come. All you have to do is maintain the relationship. This is the essence of building oil wells in your business.

There is simply no better way to get business than through repeat and referred customers, and affiliate relationships with other businesses will generate a steady stream of referrals at very low (or zero) cost. But it's important that you take the long view. Building affiliate relationships takes time. In comparison, it's far easier to run an ad on Facebook or in the newspaper than it is to build a relationship. But the rewards of an affiliate relationship are much, much bigger. In my opinion, if you want to maximize your success, affiliate relationships with other businesses are no longer a luxury. This is because consumers are more standoffish, distrusting, and price sensitive than ever before. When you get a referral from another business, you go in on borrowed trust. It's a shortcut to overcoming the tremendous price resistance you encounter with total strangers who visit your business because they saw an ad, your website, or your sign.

Yes, digging oil wells takes time and effort, but by having an on-purpose, step-by-step strategy for building affiliates, it's possible to do it very quickly. By using a simple, three-step strategy, I developed over a dozen affiliate relationships in 90 days. Eight of the 11 local flooring dealers and furniture stores referred my carpet cleaning company, along with Realtors, interior designers, dry cleaners, and contractors. Lots of oil wells.

A Three-Step Process To Quickly Establish Affiliate Relationships Without Cold-Calling

Step 1: Send them something unusual in the mail. Never call a business owner cold to make an affiliate proposal. First send them an unusual-looking proposal letter. The key to making this strategy work is to make sure your letter gets opened and read. Here are two simple tricks to make sure both happen:

Get Your Letters Opened And Read

Realize that up to 60% of "junk mail" gets thrown out unopened. How many times have you pulled a stack of mail out of your mailbox, and then stood next to a trash can throwing away the junk mail? We all do this. So if you don't want the same thing to happen to your letter it shouldn't look like a mailer from a business; it should look like personal correspondence. To do this, hand-write the address on a plain envelope, not business stationery. Your return address should also be hand-written and not contain your business name. Use real, live, honest-to-gosh first-class stamps, not metered mail. No one sends personal correspondence using metered mail. I call this a "stealth mailer." Virtually 100% of stealth mailers get opened. They also tend to get opened first. Again, imagine you're sorting your mail over a trash can and you come across a plain envelope with a hand-written address and return address, and a first-class stamp. Are you going to ignore it for days or weeks? Odds are you'll probably open it right away.

Now that they've opened your letter, you have about three seconds to capture their attention and make sure it gets read. In this case I'll staple a one-dollar bill to the top of the letter. This is called a "grabber." Ask yourself this: If you got a letter with real money stapled to the top, would you toss it without reading it?

Step 2: Follow-up call. The one-and-only purpose of the phone call is to set up a meeting with the business owner. Don't make any kind of affiliate proposal during this call.

Step 3: Meet with them in person. If possible, take them to coffee or lunch. This gives you a chance to meet without business distractions. Your goal for the meeting is to determine if they are going to be a good fit for a referral relationship. Assuming you want to work with this business you will then take steps to solidify and maintain the relationship.

Maintain The Relationship

You've just dug an oil well that will continue to produce for years to come, provided you dig the well deep and maintain it. Here are some tips for doing that:

- Within a week of your meeting with the business owner, stop by their place of business with a box of cookies or pastries. If they have a staff, be sure to meet everyone. I've found that if there is staff, they will send most of the referrals because they are often the ones dealing with the public. It pays to make friends with the staff.

- Leave business cards and a card holder that can be displayed on their front counter or their desk. Include copies of your consumer's guide or free report.

- Subscribe the owner and each member of their staff to your monthly newsletter. Everyone is sent a copy. This way they are hearing from you each and every month.

- Give them periodic "bribes." Cookies, pastries, pizza, Chinese food, Starbucks, etc. How often they get the bribes—and how large of a bribe—is directly proportional to how much business they send. (If you send in lunch, make sure you let them know ahead of time.) I've even sent out letters saying that for every third or fourth referral they send that turns into a customer, I'll send in lunch for the entire staff. For the businesses that are sending you a steady stream of customers, take something to them every month. Others might get something only at Christmas. It all depends. Remember: It's a relationship.

- Meet periodically with the business owner for lunch or coffee to deepen the relationship. How often depends upon the profitability of the relationship, how willing they seem to work with you, their character, how they treat your customers, etc.

- As time goes by and your relationship deepens, you can propose various joint marketing strategies. Some I propose right away, some I wait until I get to know them better.

The thing to keep in mind is that you are building relationships, and this goes both ways. You want to be sure that you're dealing with someone you can trust, as well as giving them a chance to trust you.

Two Kinds Of Affiliate Relationships

There are two kinds of relationships with affiliates: exclusive and non-exclusive.

Exclusive

This means that you only work with one business owner in a particular business category. For example, you might choose to work with only one interior designer. The biggest benefit of this kind of relationship is you refer each other exclusively to your respective customer databases. For example, you can write articles for each other's newsletters, do joint promotions, carry each other's literature in your places of business, etc. The drawback is you lock out the possibility of working with all the other interior designers.

Non-Exclusive

This means you work with several business owners in a particular business category. The advantage is you can have multiple income streams from a single industry. The disadvantage is you have to be careful about how you promote and refer these businesses; otherwise, you jeopardize the relationships.

For example, I had eight different flooring dealers referring my carpet cleaning company. They and their employees all got my newsletter. If I had allowed one of them to write an article in my newsletter, it would have caused problems. Therefore, if I was going to let one of them write an article, I had to give all the dealers a chance to do the same thing. Usually I just never opened that can of worms.

The other thing I was careful about was referring customers who needed floor covering. When a customer asked who I recommended, I always asked where they got their flooring. If it was one of the eight, I would refer them back to that company. Otherwise, I would rotate which company I referred. But I was always fair.

Also, in a non-exclusive relationship I could never promote a particular flooring store to MY customer database. Remember: All eight stores were referring their customers to me. If I promoted a particular store, I would effectively be sending the customers of the other seven stores to the store I was promoting. Not good for building long-term, trusting relationships.

Things to consider

Should you go exclusive or non-exclusive? There is no right or wrong answer. I did it both ways. Before developing an exclusive relationship, make absolutely sure of two things: that they will treat your customers like gold, and they are open to creative, joint-marketing strategies.

Many times the relationship will evolve from non-exclusive to exclusive. For example, I had three or four interior designers referring my business. Eventually one of them became my "champion," referring many customers, giving me access to their database, etc. That relationship morphed into an exclusive partnership.

When establishing exclusive relationships, generally the benefit for both of you is promoting your businesses to each other's customers. One dealer I coached had an exclusive relationship with an interior designer. He sent his monthly newsletter to her list of 1,500 past customers. Each issue included a short article written by the designer and her contact information. The dealer paid for the entire thing. He benefitted because he got to market directly to her list, and the designer benefitted by getting free advertising. He made hundreds-of-thousands of dollars with this arrangement.

Affiliate "Massive Action"

Instead of picking one business at a time, pick 5-10 businesses you think you would like to partner with. Call each of the businesses and get the name of the owner. Send your intro letter. Follow up 3-5 days later with a phone call. Set up a meeting. This is how I started over a dozen affiliate relationships in just a few months.

Business Categories For Affiliate Partners

- Interior designers
- Contractors
- Realtors
- Insurance agents
- Carpet cleaners
- Furniture stores
- Cabinet shops
- Window covering stores
- Paint stores
- Appliance stores
- House cleaning companies
- Janitorial companies
- Landscape maintenance

- Plumbers
- Pest control
- Veterinarians
- Pet shops
- Gift shops
- Welcome Wagon types of businesses
- Gift basket shops
- Restaurants

FIFTEEN

....

WHY SELLING ON CHEAP PRICE
IS A SUICIDE MISSION

FLOOR DEALER: We have to keep our margins low to compete with the home stores.

JIM: So, how can I help you?

FLOOR DEALER: Well, we're going broke.

"We're kicking Home Depot's butt!"

I was on the phone with Mark Bouquet, a floor dealer from the suburbs of Chicago.

"We're kicking Home Depot's butt. We love having them as neighbors because we take a lot of business from them."

I spewed iced tea as I burst out laughing. "Details! Details! Give me details!" I said after I picked myself up off the floor. (I just *love* a good Home Depot story.) He went on to tell me that they get lots of people into their store who had previously visited the "Big Orange Giant," which is just down the road from his showroom. A large percentage of them wind up buying from him even though his prices are higher.

What was going on here? That shouldn't be possible! The only thing that people care about is who has the lowest price, right? Tragically, too many dealers cling to this myth, bemoaning the cheapness of the buying public with the pathos of a Shakespearean actor. But the idea that people only care about price is simply not true. If it were, everyone would eat only at McDonald's and the only cars you'd see on the road would be Kia compacts. So the first secret in commanding premium prices is to realize price is *not* the only consideration in your prospect's mind.

It's painful but important to realize that selling on price is the lazy way out. Any yahoo can run through their showroom like a rabid monkey, marking stuff down in order to move product. It takes no imagination, no effort, no skill. But selling at premium prices? With a box store down the street? Ah, now that requires *real* marketing and selling skill. So the second secret is realizing that charging premium prices is not about luck; it's about skill. And that's extremely good news because, while you don't have control over luck (or if a big, mean ol' box store saunters into your neighborhood and kicks sand in your face and makes you cry), you *do* have control over increasing your skills in sales and marketing. Then you can kick sand right back—faster and harder—like my friend Mark does.

The third secret is to realize that when you compete on price, you have nowhere to go but down. If your big marketing advantage is being the lowest priced, all it takes is for some knucklehead to sell at a cheaper price (sometimes at a loss just to get the sale) and you've just lost your advantage.

Live By Price, Die By Price

Conversely, if you learn to successfully market yourself as the "premium service and price" dealer, like many floor dealers I've taught, then you have nowhere to go but up. While your competitors are fighting for the scraps, you'll be enjoying nice, high margins, and the accompanying wealth that this allows, never worrying about becoming a casualty of the "price wars" going on all around you. Case in point: Recently, Mark generated over $3 million in revenue, a record for his business, and this after nearly closing his doors a few years before. During this time three of his direct competitors, including a national chain, went out of business. Steve, another dealer, used savvy sales and marketing to survive the recession, and as a result has scooped up the market share left behind by his failed competitors. He's busier than ever, a result of the vacuum left behind by (former) dealers in his market who bit the dust. Last man standing.

Watch Out! You Won't Make It Up In Volume

The fourth secret is to realize that you will not make up for low price with higher volume. Most businesses go bankrupt in the midst of higher gross sales, but lower margins. I'll bet you the biggest lobster in Maine that the dealers from Steve's and Mark's neighborhoods who went under did so in the midst of slashing their prices. More casualties of "price wars."

No One Buys On Price Alone

Walmart, Home Depot, Lowe's, and a host of other giant corporations have spent years and billions of dollars spreading the "cheap-price" gospel, that the most important consideration in making a buying decision is who has the lowest price. To a great degree they've been successful in brainwashing consumers that price is the biggest consideration.

Again, it's important to realize that no one buys on price alone. Even the most die-hard price shopper who wants to buy tan Berber carpet will not opt for hot-pink shag just because it's cheaper. Admittedly, this is an extreme example, but it makes the point that price is not the only consideration in *anyone's* mind, even if the consumers themselves think so. Larry Steinmetz often speaks to the sales forces of large companies on this topic. He'll ask the audience members to raise their hands if they only consider price when buying a shirt. A few hands always go up. He'll then ask if they would buy the shirt if it was too small, or it had huge holes in it, or was purple with pink polka dots. All the hands go back down.

The key to selling at premium prices is engineering a zero-resistance selling environment, which includes creating differentiation from your competitors so your prospects are no longer comparing apples to apples. Now, if you fail to differentiate yourself from your competitors—in the way you market, talk to walk-ins, answer phones, in your selling process, etc.—then you'll never escape the cheap-price rat race of doom. Your only consolation will be to say to yourself what all dealers say who are trapped in the low-price rat race: People only care about *cheap price*. That's cold consolation, especially considering that by clinging to this myth you're depriving yourself of greater profits, easier selling (yes, selling gets easier when your prices are high), and a more pleasurable and peaceful business. Not to mention enjoying your *Ideal Lifestyle*, building wealth, and having a great retirement.

Scraping The Bottom Of The Barrel

Years ago in my hometown there was a charity selling coupon books with deep discounts to local businesses such as restaurants, lube shops, and—you guessed it—carpet cleaning companies. One carpet cleaner participated by including a coupon for "one room free, up to 200 sq. ft." He nearly went broke from all the bargain hunters who hired him to clean only a single room but no other areas of their house or apartment. He showed up at one "couponer's" home and found she had used masking tape to mark off the 200 sq. ft. so there would be no chance of having to pay him anything.

And that's the problem with daily deal-type advertising in a nutshell. It magnetically attracts price shoppers like a 10-ton magnet attracts paper clips. Many businesses—especially restaurants—that used Groupon reported hordes of customers showing up to take advantage of the deep discounts, never to return and purchase at regular prices. *Forbes* reported that a restaurant in Portland, Oregon, lost so much money on a Groupon deal that it would have gone out of business had it not secured a loan to cover its losses.

Let's not forget about Home Depot's infamous "Free Installation" offer. Actually it's not an offer, it's a lie: No installer will work for nothing. The difference in cost is added to the materials. It also devalues the critical importance of quality installation by a skilled technician. Do not, under any circumstances, give in to the temptation to sink to Home Depot's level with a similar offer. When someone tells a dealer, "Home Depot will install it for free," I teach dealers to say, "Great! You've come to the right place. We fix free installations."

I produce and co-host *Floor Covering News'* Marketing Mastery webinars. During one of them I polled the attendees and asked how many of them were using "cheap-price" language on their websites, such as "our prices won't be beat," or "highest quality at the lowest prices." A number of them said they did, including a dealer who said he "had to" in order to compete. Unfortunately, many dealers feel this way, which is tragic because it's simply not true. But lacking good marketing and sales training, these dealers don't know what else to do, so out of desperation they copy the "low-ball" strategies they see their competitors using.

If you promote on cheap price, you create enormous problems for yourself:

- You magnetically attract "bottom feeders." (Who'da thought?) You're scraping the bottom of the barrel.

- Not only are you making less (going broke?), but price shoppers are genetically programmed to complain and cause problems.

- When your margins are too thin, you simply cannot afford to provide the kind of world-class service that generates referrals. (Except referrals to other bottom feeders who complain a lot. Terrific.)

- If your market advantage is selling at the lowest price, and someone comes along and offers an even lower price, you've instantly lost your advantage. Live by price, die by price.

- Very few dealers prosper by slashing their prices. By doing so, you stack the odds that you'll: 1) go out of business; or 2) toil away for decades dealing with the worst-of-the-worst customers, always struggling financially.

And that's just the tip of the "problems-caused-by-cheap-price" iceberg. Over and over again I've seen flooring retailers desperately trying to figure out how to sell their products for the *least* money. This is Walmart thinking, 180 degrees out of whack. You should devote your time, energy, and money to figuring out how to sell your products for the *most* money.

When I was in college I earned my daily bread by giving private guitar lessons at a music store. The owner of this store was a good-hearted and generous fellow. A little too generous. He sold his wares at incredibly thin margins, so thin that he had to take part-time work outside his store to stay afloat, always had to do things on the cheap, and could never get ahead. His excuse was the same as many floor dealers: *The only thing people care about is cheap price.* That was many years ago, and things haven't changed much for him. He still struggles. His business doesn't prosper.

That's a heavy, heavy price to pay for selling things cheaply. Not only does it hinder your ability to grow your business, but you suffer personally through the inability to save for retirement, take vacations, and simply enjoy life. Life is a constant struggle. Too many floor dealers can relate.

Walmart can sell things cheaply because they are set up to move a ton of products, so they make it up in volume. Flooring retail doesn't work that way; you will not make it up in volume. Yes, there are a handful of national dealers that have adopted the Walmart model and seem to be succeeding ... for now. But cheap price is a fragile market advantage because all it takes is for someone to figure out how to sell at an even cheaper price and you've instantly lost your advantage, and quite possibly your business. There was a time when Kmart ruled the cheap-price retail kingdom. Thirty years ago it was inconceivable that they could be knocked from their throne. Then Walmart came along. If they aren't careful they'll suffer the same fate. Other discount boxes, not to mention online retailers, have been carving up the cheap-price retail market and stealing market share from Walmart. An April 2013 editorial in *Forbes* by Rick Ungar has the telling title: *Walmart Pays Workers Poorly And Sinks While Costco Pays Workers Well And Sails—Proof That You Get What You Pay For.* Costco's earnings for year-on-year sales were at 8% while Walmart's were at 1.2%. Walmart pays its workers horrible wages and is grossly understaffed, resulting in a lack of customer help in the stores and an overall customer experience that is terrible and getting worse. Ungar theorizes that this has driven customers to Costco. I think he's right. But that's what happens when cheap price is your driving force; little things like customer service get kicked to the curb.

What About Successful Discount Dealers?

You might be thinking about the national discount dealers that seem to be succeeding on a cheap-price model. Here are some facts to consider:

In order to succeed in the cheap-price game, you've got to have a business plan in place that supports selling at a discount, which means having the economy of mass scale working for you so you can *purchase* at a discount. The vast majority of dealers who try to compete on price don't have a low-price business model in place: They are being reactionary, acting out of desperation. How can you tell which you are? If you simply go through you showroom marking down price tags then you don't have a business plan.

Next, go to www.ConsumerAffairs.com, www.RipoffReport.com, and other review sites and search "Empire Flooring," "Home Depot Flooring," "Lumber Liquidators," and other national discounters. Then do a Google search of flooring reviews for the same discounters. If you haven't done this before your jaw will drop at the hundreds of horror stories posted by furious consumers. This is the inevitable result of Walmart-style selling. You can't afford to provide top-notch customer service, you can't afford to honor your warranties, and you can't afford to pay your installers well.

Finally, don't forget the Kmart story. In the early 1980's no one could imagine them being knocked off their cheap-price throne ... until Walmart came along and mopped up the floor with them. These national flooring discounters are vulnerable to the same fate.

Get Out Now

If you're a retailer I urge you to completely get out of the cheap-price rat race. I've taught many dealers to sell at premium prices, and to do so in every conceivable market, from big cities to tiny agricultural towns and everywhere in between. Dealers from across the U.S. and Canada have proven you can sell at premium prices in *any* market and in *any* economy, even right across the street from Home Depot. Anyone can learn, but it starts with a willingness to adopt a different mindset and to implement new sales and marketing strategies.

I wonder how the music store owner's business and life would have been different if he'd devoted his energies into figuring out how to sell his products for the *most* money. I wonder the same thing about floor dealers who are trying to compete on cheap price.

As discussed, a cheap-price business model is difficult to maintain even for large companies that have a carefully laid out plan in place for selling at thin margins. They can buy in bulk, and have usually secured deep discounts with manufacturers and vendors. They may be publicly traded, or have significant investor capital, or large cash reserves, or some combination of these, thus enabling them to sustain losses longer than small businesses in order to grab market share.

Here's a critical question if you're selling on cheap price: *Do you have this infrastructure for mass scale in place?* If not, then you need to think very carefully about your business plan. The vast majority of dealers who resort to cheap-price selling aren't in the position described above. They do it because they feel like they "have to in order to compete." Their pricing strategy isn't a *strategy* at all; it's totally reactionary. Under these conditions, the dealer who sells on cheap price has embarked on a suicide mission that virtually guarantees that they will either: 1) slowly go broke; or 2) struggle forever.

*It is not the crook in modern business that we fear, but the honest man
who doesn't know what he is doing.   —Owen D. Young*

Honest dealers who don't know what they are doing copy the pricing of the big companies. Other dealers copy the copycats. Eventually it becomes a giant game of the blind-and-dumb leading the blind-and-dumb, until you get what we have now: the vast majority of flooring advertising—websites, display ads, mailers, everything—resorting to cheap price.

Many dealers are looking for that magic, silver bullet: a single campaign or sales trick or ad that will enable them to escape the cheap-price rat race. Sorry to break the bad news, but there are no silver bullets. To sell at premium prices in a discounted world you must employ multiple sales and marketing strategies, all working together and reinforcing one another. You might be thinking, "But, Jim, that sounds hard!" Yup. But what's harder: learning to sell at premium prices, or struggling for years and possibly going broke trying to sell on the cheap?

*Life's hard when you live it the easy way; easy when you
live it the hard way.   —David Kekich*

The Lumber Liquidators Scandal

As we were getting ready to go to publication with this book, the Lumber Liquidators story broke on 60 Minutes. It turns out that Lumber Liquidators had been selling Chinese-made laminate flooring with formaldehyde levels up to 13 times higher than allowed by California emissions standards. Formaldehyde is found in virtually everything, living or manufactured, but excessive emissions can cause health problems, which is why California has strict standards for the amount allowed in flooring. Products following these standards are known as CARB 2 compliant. CARB 2 standards have been accepted by the U.S. Congress.

It is estimated that in California alone tens of thousands of Lumber Liquidators customers were victimized.

In two of my *Marketing Mastery* columns for *Floor Covering News*, I addressed the Lumber Liquidators issue. I thought I'd end this chapter with a reprint of one of those articles.

NEWSPAPER floor covering news

marketing mastery

Lumber Liquidators and the Cheap-Price Suicide Mission

I've preached numerous times in this column that for most dealers, competing on price is a dead-end suicide mission. If you wondered if I was over-stating my case, the Lumber Liquidators debacle should forever erase that idea from your mind.

JIM AUGUSTUS ARMSTRONG

Positioning yourself in the market as the cheap-price leader is at best a fragile, temporary market advantage. The reason is all it takes is for someone to come along with a cheaper price and you've instantly lost your advantage. Companies like Lumber Liquidators that have built their entire business around low price know this, and they face enormous pressure to keep their prices down. This pressure often leads to poor quality control, and sometimes to activities that are unethical or outright illegal.

Customer service is another casualty of cheap price. It's simply not possible to give good service, provide quality installations, or honor your warranties when you're charging razor thin margins. Do an online search for customer reviews for Lumber Liquidators, Home Depot, Empire, or any other major discounter and you will find hundreds of horror stories.

A cheap-price business model is difficult to maintain even for large companies that can buy in bulk, have investor capitol, and cash reserves. In the early 1980's Kmart was the king of the low-price retailers, and in their heyday the idea that they could be dethroned seemed ludicrous. Then Walmart came along.

However, most dealers engaging in price slashing don't have an actual cheap-price business plan in place, or the economies of mass scale working for them. They are acting out of pure desperation, reacting to the advertising they see coming from the national discounters. They feel like they have to lower their prices in order to be "competitive." Here's how to tell if you fall into this category: If all you're doing is lowering the numbers on your price tags, you're most likely a "desperate price slasher."

Desperate price slashers also pay an enormous personal cost. They are typically overworked and severely underpaid. 50+ hour work weeks are the norm, and much of that time is spent dealing with the problems created by selling on the cheap: inability to hire quality installers and sales people, lack of administrative help (they can't afford it), robbing Peter to pay Paul, customer complaints, and so on. Sometimes they work for decades and have nothing to show for their effort except a business that's not saleable (who would want to buy it?), little or no retirement savings, and a pile of debt.

So what is the solution? How can dealers command margins of 45% and higher when legions of competitors are pushing cheap price? The solution is to use a system of strategies all working together to empower you to command premium prices. There is no silver bullet, no single strategy that will make this happen, so the first step is to make a commitment to learning and implementing multiple premium-price strategies. In the next installment I'll review a number of proven strategies to help you do that. In the meantime, I'll leave you with a premium-price strategy you can implement immediately: *consumer education.* My last column was titled *How Consumers Can Protect Themselves From Unethical Floor Dealers*, and was written as a consumer education piece in response to the Lumber Liquidators scandal. It includes five steps a consumer can take to find an honest, ethical dealer who sells safe, quality products. I designed this as a sales tool for dealers to give out to their customers who ask about Lumber Liquidators or the safety of laminate flooring. It educates customers and positions dealers as consumer advocates, a powerful premium-price strategy.

For free reprints email us at Support@FlooringSuccessSystems.com.

....

SIXTEEN

HOW TO CREATE A ZERO-RESISTANCE SELLING ENVIRONMENT

FLOOR DEALER: I can't sell at high prices because in my town the only thing people care about is cheap price.

JIM: There's a floor dealer three blocks away from you who has been in business for 20 years selling at premium prices. How do you explain that?

FLOOR DEALER: Uh …

The 80/10/10 Rule Of Pricing

It's useless for me to give you premium-pricing strategies if you have a mindset that says, "The only thing my customers care about is cheap price." So let's begin by serving up some delicious, multigrain, zero-calorie, organic *brain food*.

First, train your brain that you are worth it. I coach dealers on how to command premium prices, and this usually involves working on their self-image. If your self-image says you don't deserve to get high prices, you'll self-sabotage.

Unconsciously, many entrepreneurs feel guilty about charging high prices, or they think they don't deserve it. Don't be too quick to dismiss this as psychobabble. If you find yourself constantly getting beat up on price, there is an excellent chance you are unconsciously creating this situation. No amount of training in the *techniques* of sales and marketing will solve this problem until the underlying mindset is changed. An excellent book on this subject is *Psycho-Cybernetics* by Dr. Maxwell Maltz. It was written in the 1960's, and the principles it teaches are the foundation of most current-day self-improvement training.

Next, train your brain that the customer service of Home Depot, Empire, and Lumber Liquidators stinks like an overflowing septic tank. They have absolutely no unique product offerings, and Home Depot's flooring "expert" one week may have been their plumbing "expert" the week before. Therefore, their only competitive advantage is cheap price. Other than that they've quite literally got nothing to offer.

Finally, train your brain that if the only thing people cared about was cheap price, then everyone would eat at McDonald's and drive a Kia. In fact, you can divide the entire population into roughly three groups: 80/10/10. The bottom 10% are die-hard price-shopping bottom feeders, hardwired to always buy the lowest priced product. They also tend to be the biggest complainers, impossible to please.

You *do not* want these people as customers. Send them to your competitors. (Gift-wrapped, with a nice bow.)

The top 10% are hardwired for highest quality. They want the best and they are willing to pay for it.

The middle 80% also want quality, and they are generally willing to pay for it provided you educate them on how they will benefit by paying more. Education-based marketing is an important part of creating a zero-resistance selling environment.

What Environment Means For Floor Dealers

en·vi·ron·ment: the aggregate of surrounding things,
conditions, or influences

There is no such thing as a single strategy that will magically enable you to command premium prices, so fuggedaboudit! Instead, your job is to use multiple strategies and techniques—all working together and reinforcing each other—to create a zero-resistance selling *environment*. Every touch point—your ads and website, your customer's visit to your store, your sales process, the way the phones are answered—should contribute to this environment. I teach more than 27 strategies to do this, and in this chapter we're going to look at a handful of effective elements to create *your* zero-resistance environment.

Positioning Yourself As A Trusted Advisor

Imagine someone going to the doctor because she suspects she might have brain cancer, and before the doctor begins the examination she says, "I was looking online and I found another doctor who will do an examination for $49.95. Your receptionist says you charge $120. Is that the best you can do?" And when he gives her his recommendations for treatment, she replies, "Well, I was talking to my sister-in-law the other day and she says I should do something different." It wouldn't happen. Why? Because the patient sees the doctor as a Trusted Advisor. Also, getting cured of cancer is probably a much higher priority to her than getting the cheapest price.

Yet how many times have you had customers question your price and your recommendations? It happens all the time to floor dealers. There are a lot of reasons for this, but one of the big ones is *bad positioning*. Because they don't know better, many dealers inadvertently position themselves more like a "used car dealer" rather than a Trusted Advisor.

A "used car salesman" chases people down, has nothing special to offer (other than a "great deal," which translates to selling by price), and is generally not respected or trusted. He makes his living by pressuring people through hard-sell techniques, much like the proverbial vacuum salesman who sticks his foot in the door and won't take "no" for an answer.

Doctors have a specific process

Let's say you've got an ear infection and it's hurting like the devil. Do you just drive to your doctor's office, walk inside, and stroll back to the exam area and start chatting with him? Probably not. First, you call to make an appointment and hope they can fit you in this week. When you arrive you sign in, then you wait in the waiting room for the better part of an hour, then you go to the exam room where a nurse's assistant takes your blood pressure, temperature, etc. Then she leaves and you wait some more. Once the doctor finally arrives, he starts by asking you questions, and then he does an exam. Then, and only then, do you get a prescription.

I'm not suggesting that you put your customers through a grueling process like this. My point is that doctors actually *have* a process and *they* control it, not their customers. Do you have a specific sales process that you control? Or does the customer walk in and control the process? What is it costing you by not having a process you control?

Doctors won't "do anything" to get the customer to buy

Do you agree to all your customer's demands, even when they are unreasonable or fall outside of your business systems? Do you "cave in" on price? Do you allow them to control the process for fear of "chasing them off"?

Doctors don't do this. Acquiescing to all your customer's demands positions you as desperate, not as a Trusted Advisor. I'm not suggesting being totally inflexible, but many dealers go too far the other direction, and as a result position themselves as a car salesman rather than a doctor. One key to avoiding the "doing anything" syndrome is being willing to tell a customer no. It's so utterly liberating to be able to tell a stubborn or disagreeable customer that *this* is how you do it, and if they don't want to do it that way, perhaps they would be happier going down the street. (Then hand them a list of your competitors' names. I've done this.)

Doctors have compelling reasons for the customer to use them other than low price

This book is all about strategies and systems that allow you to present solid, compelling reasons for customers to choose you other than being the "cheapest." A key to success is taking a prospect through the zero-resistance process before they are shown a price.

- A customer visits your store after seeing an ad or a website full of testimonials or calling in and listening to a 24-hour FREE consumer awareness message.
- She is offered a beverage.
- She sees more testimonials and photos on your "brag" wall.
- You take her through an actual *Sales Closer System* instead of just winging it.
- You use testimonials in all your marketing and your sales process.

These are just a few of the things you can do to totally set yourself apart, and they are compelling reasons to buy from you other than price. If she begins to be difficult or demands that you do things outside of your process, you can turn her down with the confidence that you have presented her with a service that utterly blows away your competitors.

It won't happen often, but if after seeing all these compelling reasons that rare price-resistant customer still throws a low price from another dealer in your face, you can remind her of your guarantees and ask her if they offer the same thing ... in writing. You can also ask if they have given her a stack of testimonials *proving* that they honor their warranties and *proving* that they provide outstanding service. If she says "no," then ask her if it makes sense to entrust the largest interior design decision to a store that can't even provide testimonials proving that they provide excellent service and that they honor their warranties.

If someone still wants to beat you up on price (a true rarity after all this), just realize that this person is NOT your ideal customer and have fun with it. Tell her that if she is interested in cheap price, there are many other local or online dealers that can help her. As you say this, hand her a list of your competitors, including Home Depot and Lowe's. This is empowering, and a lot of fun.

Doctors don't "sell"—they give professional recommendations

What's the first thing the doctor does when you see him for the first time? Does he stroll into the exam room with a big grin and say, "Hey, we've got penicillin on special, 25% off! And we've got a 2 for 1 deal on Viagra, today only!" It doesn't happen.

Instead, doctors sit down with your file and ask you a series of questions related to your health. They find out what your specific needs are. They then have the ability to give their professional recommendations. You should do the same thing.

Doctors don't permit violation of their personal or professional time—limited access

If you own a mobile showroom, this is a perfect opportunity to promote the idea that you "work by appointment only." This is a powerful positioning tool because all highly paid, respected professionals work by "appointment only." Doctors, CPA's, financial planners, and high-end interior designers are never instantly "available." You have to make an appointment and sometimes it takes weeks to see them! Does this hurt their business? Far from it! It creates the perception that they are in high demand and that their service is highly valuable.

So if you have a mobile showroom, use "by appointment only" to help create the perception that you are in high demand, and that your services are highly valuable; after all, they are!

Watch Out!

Don't Sell At A Discount Just Because You Run A Mobile Showroom

I see mobile showroom operators do this a lot, but it's a mistake. Your prices should be at least as high as a retail location. After all, you're providing a convenience to your customers. Most high-priced designers don't have a showroom. Do they discount because of this? Nope, and neither should you.

If you don't have a mobile showroom, there are several things you can do to create the perception that you are in demand and that your service is valuable. First, when a customer comes into your store, take control of the process and take her through a *Sales Closer System*. This immediately lets the customer know that you aren't desperate. Second, providing lots of testimonials proves that you are in demand. Third, when it comes time to schedule the in-home visit, you *are* working by appointment only. The trick here is *not* to say, "I'm available all this week. When is a good time for you?" This makes you sound too available and not in demand. Instead say, "We're in high demand, and typically we're booked out for 2-3 weeks. Let me see when our next opening is. Are mornings or afternoons better for you?" Then give them two appointment options based on what they tell you. "I have one next Tuesday at 3:30 or Wednesday at 2:15. Which is better for you?" *Key Point:* Do this even if your calendar is *totally empty*! I ALWAYS use scripts and train my staff to do and say the same thing. After walking a customer through this exact script they'll take just about any opening I have available.

Another key is to decide your schedule ahead of time and then stick to it. For example, if you only want to do in-home visits two afternoons and one morning each week, block these out in your calendar and stick with it. When it comes time to schedule the appointment, if they want a morning slot, say "Wednesdays are when I do morning appointments. I have an 8:30 or an 11:00. Which is better for you?"

Apply this to your personal schedule as well. If you don't work weekends, then don't allow a customer to pressure you into a weekend appointment. After all, you're not only building your *Ideal Business*, but also your *Ideal Lifestyle*. Don't allow customers to rob you of that.

I have done this for years and I rarely, rarely ever lose a customer by sticking to my guns. And the occasional customer that I do lose is generally a demanding, pushy, inconsiderate person I don't want as a customer anyway. Having a set of standards and procedures by which you conduct business not only positions you correctly, it acts as a filter to screen out the customers you don't want. Bonus!

Doctors act in the customer's best interest

First of all, this does *not* mean allowing a customer to violate your time, and it does not mean charging a cheap price. Doctors—in general—do a good job acting in their customer's best interest, but good luck finding a doctor who will allow you to violate his professional or personal time, and beat him up on price. And if you do manage to find a doctor who allows this, do you really want him doing brain surgery on you??

One way to act in the customer's best interest is by making quality recommendations. Again, asking lots of questions and writing down the answers before making product recommendations does a couple of things: 1) It demonstrates to the customer that you intend to act in her best interest; and 2) it gives you the information you need to close the sale. It also means being honest, even when it costs you a little in the short term. For example, you get an order of carpet and pad in, but discover that the padding is a lower grade than the customer wanted. It would be very easy to go ahead and install the lower grade without telling the customer. A dealer that acts in the customer's best interest will handle this by: 1) calling the customer and letting her know what has happened and that there will be a delay; and 2) giving *her* the option to choose the lower grade at a reduced price, or wait for the other to arrive.

This is really a character issue. If you truly care about your customer's best interest, it will be easy for you to implement the tools and strategies to fulfill that promise. If you don't care about your customer's best interest—if you're willing to do things that would benefit you but harm your customer—then you need to shift your values or you'll always struggle.

By applying the lessons learned from doctors and used car salesmen, you will position yourself as a Trusted Advisor, be respected, and have the power to charge higher prices than your competitors.

The Doctor Vs. The Used Car Salesman

Doctor	Used Car Salesman
Customer comes to him—does not behave desperately	Chases customer—or behaves so desperately that he creates the appearance of chasing
Has a specific process that he and his staff control	Has no process—allows customer too much control
Won't "do anything" to get the customer to "buy"—not desperate	WILL do anything to "make a deal"—prostitutes himself
Has compelling reasons for the customer to use him—he is "the" expert (This takes price out of the equation.)	Has ZERO compelling reasons to use him versus his competitors—entire transaction is a price game
Doesn't "sell"—gives professional recommendations	Is constantly "selling" (pressuring)
Does not permit violation of his personal time or business time—limited access	Is "always available"—even gives out his cell and home phone numbers
Takes the time to ask questions to find out what his customer needs	Doesn't care what his customer needs—only what he can "sell" her
Acts in his customer's best interest	Acts in his own best interest
Giving—mostly concerned with what's best for his customer—it shows	Selfish—mostly concerned with bamboozling his customer—it shows

As a result ...	As a result ...
Is seen as a Trusted Advisor	Is viewed as a "salesman"—not trusted
Price is generally not an issue—can name his price	Price is the only issue—must always beat the other dealer's price
Respected	Not respected
Comes across as genuine and an expert	Comes across like a midway "carny"
Has a relationship with his customer	No relationship
Repeat and referral business happens regularly and automatically	Repeat and referral business is a rarity
Builds a large, faithful clientele who literally are clients for life—does not depend on walk-in traffic. Has a "practice"	No clientele—makes his entire living hoping for walk-in traffic

"But, Jim, My Customers Will Buy From My Competitors If I Do That!"

Some dealers are so petrified of losing a sale that they'll make a number of mistakes that position themselves as desperate:

- Allowing customers to abuse their time
- Caving in on price
- Letting the customer control the sales process
- Being "instantly available" whenever a customer wants to communicate with them
- Allowing customers to cause stress in their business and life

Do you want to be respected or abused?

You need to look yourself in the mirror and honestly answer this question. Some dealers say they want to be respected, but their actions scream "Abuse me!" to their customers. Look, you want to have a long, prosperous, successful, rewarding, non-stressful career in flooring, right? Well, this can't happen if you don't command respect from your customers. If you constantly cave on price, allow abuses of your time, and let the customer control the sales process, then you are guaranteeing yourself a stressful, unprofitable, non-rewarding, and possibly short career in flooring.

So the first thing you've got to do is decide, once and for all, that you *will not* be abused, that you are committed to positioning yourself and your sales team as Trusted Advisors. I can show you the strategies to position yourself as a respected, Trusted Advisor (instead of a used car salesman), but it begins with a commitment on your part to make this happen.

Which restaurant would you choose?

Let's say you want to take your spouse out to dinner to celebrate your 25th wedding anniversary. Would you choose a restaurant that has an empty parking lot, no wait, and a nearly empty dining area simply because they can seat you immediately and the food is cheap? Or would you rather go to a high-priced restaurant that is impossible to get in without making a reservation at least two weeks in advance, and is always packed? Remember, this is your 25th anniversary, a very special date that doesn't happen every week. You're going to be making a memory that will last a lifetime. Which restaurant will you have the most confidence in to deliver that memory of a lifetime? Most people—especially the kind of customers you want—will choose the second option.

Getting flooring is special; it doesn't happen every week. It's one of the biggest interior design expenditures your customers will make. Flooring will "make or break" the rest of the décor. The flooring type has a big impact on the indoor health of the home. Buying new flooring should be given the same kind of respect as that 25th anniversary dinner. If you: 1) position yourself as a Trusted Advisor; 2) create total differentiation from your competition; 3) use education-based marketing so your customers know exactly why they should choose you over every other option; and 4) engineer your sales and marketing process so that customers independently arrive at the conclusion that they'd have to be crazy to buy from anyone else, even if they're cheaper, then you have put yourself in the position of the second, exclusive restaurant. This is absolutely possible to do, as evidenced by the many dealers highlighted in this book.

Let's say you need brain surgery. If it's not an emergency that requires immediate attention to save your life, do you want the surgeon who can fit you in immediately and has the cheapest fee? Or do you want the highest priced, most respected surgeon who has to "squeeze you in" next month?

You *will* lose some customers ... but who cares?

Remember the 80/10/10 rule of pricing. About 10% of consumers are hardwired to buy on cheap price. No matter how great your products, services, and warranties, they want the cheapest price. You can implement every zero-resistance strategy in this book and it won't make any difference. Well, who cares? These types are genetically predisposed to be the biggest complainers, cause the most headaches, and be the slowest to pay. You *don't* want them. They are *not* your ideal customer. When you discover you are dealing with one of these "bottom 10-percenters," immediately tell them that you won't be able to help them, and hand them a list of your competitors.

You'll make a lot more money, and have more fun doing it.

The fact is, by positioning yourself as a Trusted Advisor (like a family doctor rather than a used car salesman) you will be more profitable, less stressed, and your business will be much more enjoyable for everyone involved, including your sales people. I've seen it in my own businesses and I've seen hundreds of dealers do it in their businesses. We are surrounded by the Neiman Marcuses of the world, examples of businesses that successfully command respect and high prices. We are also surrounded by the Walmarts of the world, scraping the bottom of the barrel. You have to decide which you want to be.

Develop A Self-Image Of Success

Your customers will largely accept whatever value you place on your products and services. Likewise, they will also accept whatever level of expertise that you position yourself as having. Many of the strategies in this book will help you position yourself as the expert and establish respect with your prospects. However, your success at this greatly depends upon your self-image.

Develop an unwavering conviction, way down deep in your gut, that you are *worth it*. Cultivate the belief that what you are offering has tremendous value, *and that you are worth a high price*. If you have trouble believing this, say this phrase out loud 20 times each morning: *I am an expert in flooring, my products and services provide great value, and I'm worth a high price*. Write it on Post-it notes and put them on your bathroom mirror, your car dashboard, and on your computer monitor at work. This will program your mind to accept this truth. If you do it 20 times each day for 21 days, you'll program your mind to believe it.

Changing your self-image can be hard work, especially if you're trying to change deeply ingrained beliefs that are holding you back. That's why part of my coaching program for floor dealers is dedicated to helping them develop strong, healthy, success-oriented self-images. Belief in your own self-worth, or the worth of your products and services, may be a significant challenge for you. However, I promise that if you put in the effort to overcome this obstacle, you will then be able to create whatever kind of business you want, and name your price. And beyond that, create the kind of *life* you want. Developing a success-oriented self-image is worth any amount of time, energy, and money you invest because doing so will unlock doors of opportunity and success that you've never thought possible before. Conquering your own mental and emotional roadblocks to success is rarely a quick fix. It's a process. And it's not something that you have to conquer 100% before you begin to see success. As you progress, you will see results. Small at first, then larger. I urge you to make a start.

Finally, I want to say that providing floor covering services *is* tremendously valuable. A person's home is their castle, their sanctuary, their refuge from a stressed out, hectic world, and you are helping them to create that.

Never Use High-Pressure Sales Tactics
People don't like to be pressured; they like to be sold.
Flooring retail is a relationship business.

I hate it when salesmen use high-pressure tactics on me. So do you. So do your customers. That's why car salesmen are so universally disliked. They have created an entire industry based on high-pressure sales. (Not to mention unethical bait-and-switch advertising, lying, and trying to squeeze every drop of blood out of each and every customer.) That's why you should never use high-pressure to try and sell people. You may learn to get sales this way, but they will be short-lived. People will learn not to trust you.

Hard selling versus easy selling

Hard selling is the method that comes to most people's minds when they think of sales. Imagine the proverbial vacuum cleaner salesman. He goes door to door and tries to get people to buy vacuums. If they try to shut the door in his face he sticks his foot in the door and won't take "no" for an answer. He spends his time trying to talk people into a product in which they have no interest. He employs high-pressure tactics. Some people get very good at this kind of selling. But there are some serious drawbacks:

- It's very repetitive.
- It's very hard work. We are talking manual labor, cold-call grunt work. It has a high burnout factor.
- It creates a very uncomfortable selling atmosphere.
- It's an unpleasant experience.
- Prospects are suspicious.
- Prospects don't trust you.
- You are met with high skepticism.
- There is high price resistance.
- Prospects are afraid of you.
- There is a good chance they won't feel good about the experience.
- They don't like you.
- Your customers have buyer's remorse. They won't be happy with your product.
- They feel taken advantage of.
- Long-term relationships usually don't happen.

Easy selling is the opposite of hard selling, and it's the method I teach. Done properly, your prospect no longer sees you as a salesman. You are seen as a Trusted Advisor or a consultant, much like a family doctor. There are many benefits to this kind of selling:

- It's very easy.
- You are using marketing tools to do your selling for you. No repetitive manual labor or cold-call grunt work.
- It's fun!
- It creates a very comfortable selling atmosphere ... for *both* of you.
- It's a pleasant experience. Much like a chat over coffee. (I've had coffee or sodas with my prospects many times!)
- The prospect trusts you.
- You are met with very low skepticism.
- There is low price resistance.
- Prospects will feel great about the experience.
- They like you.
- There is no buyer's remorse. They'll feel great about your product or service.
- They feel like they were treated with respect.
- Easy selling opens the door for a long, happy relationship with your customer.

With easy selling 80%-90% of the sale is already made before you sit down with your prospect. The marketing tools you have in place have done all the work for you. You're not even there to "sell," but really just to agree on the details.

I've done both kinds and I'll never go back to hard selling. Easy selling is way too much fun and pleasant for everyone involved. I have developed wonderful relationships with many of my customers by using easy selling. I've been offered lunch, dinner, a glass of wine, even the use of people's swimming pools! People have told me to help myself to anything in the refrigerator, or take a break and watch TV. I have been given keys and alarm codes to people's homes. One of my customers had 300 acres with several bass ponds and a boat. She gave me the key to her gate so I could go up anytime I want and take my kids fishing. People have offered me the use of their cabins on Lake Tahoe.

This is what's possible if you develop relationships with your customers through easy selling. With hard selling none of this is ever likely to happen. No one invites a used car salesman over for dinner and a swim in their pool.

Know The Three Reasons People Don't Buy

Reason #1—They're not interested

If someone is not interested in flooring, there is seldom very much you can do to change their mind. Forget about them.

In general, your job is not to talk people who aren't interested in flooring into becoming interested. Your job is to find the people who have some level of interest already, and convince them to choose you versus your competitors, and to buy right now instead of later.

Reason #2—They can't afford you

If someone truly cannot afford your products, if they honestly don't have the money to pay for them, then they are the wrong customer. Forget about them, too.

However, this is generally a rarity, especially if you are targeting the right kinds of prospects. Usually when people say they can't afford it, or that you are too expensive, it's not because they don't have the money. They just don't believe your services are worth the money you are asking. Which brings us to the next reason people don't buy.

Reason #3—They don't believe you

When you get a prospect who says they can't afford your products, rarely, rarely, rarely is that the real reason. The fact is the vast majority your prospects *can* afford them. However, they don't believe that they are going to get a fair exchange for their money. They don't believe that you are worth it!

The challenge here is to convince your prospects that you are worth every penny (and more!). The way to convince them is to completely, thoroughly, and exhaustively educate them on the benefits of buying from you versus your competitors. To build value in their minds by building a zero-resistance selling environment.

Your own attitude will influence how prospects perceive the value of your services as well. If you don't believe you are worth it, neither will your prospects. If you are apologetic and timid about asking a high price, or you won't look them in the eye when you tell them your price, your prospects will sense this and figure that you don't really believe you are worth it either.

On the other hand, if you are confident about the superior quality of your service, and you can look your prospects in the eye, and boldly tell them about all the wonderful features of your store and your products and your service, they will sense your confidence. They will believe you are worth any price you ask. Look them in the eye and say, "The price is _____." Don't use equivocating language, such as "The price is about _____," or "The price is around _____," or "The price is normally _____."

People will largely accept whatever value you place on your service and products. If you give them a high value, so will your customers. If you put a low value on your products and services, same thing.

Remember, in most people's minds …

Low price = Low value

High price = High value

In reality, how you are perceived by your customers is completely up to you. You have the power to create whatever perception you choose.

The Power Of Reciprocity

People have an instinctive urge to reciprocate when someone gives them something for free. It's not a conscious thing, but it's there. And it's very powerful. One easy way to create a feeling of reciprocity is to offer the customer something when they visit your store. Here's how:

Offer customers a beverage. Don't say, *"Would you like something to drink?"* Because this gives them the opportunity to say "no." Instead say, *"What can I get you to drink? We have Pepsi, Diet Pepsi, Sprite, coffee, or bottled water."* By getting the customer to accept the "gift" of something as simple as a drink, they will have a tendency to feel indebted to you. They will want to reciprocate, and are therefore more likely to buy from you.

Having a sales system that leads prospects on a logical, step-by-step process from shopper to buyer also creates a feeling of indebtedness because you are spending time helping them and walking them through a series of diagnostic-type questions.

During the measure is another opportunity to create reciprocity. Ask if you can measure and inspect all the areas of flooring, not just the sections you are replacing. After you finish, write out a customized maintenance plan on how to maintain not only the floors they are purchasing from you, but the flooring they aren't having you replace. This creates even more feelings of reciprocity.

Wow 'em While You're In Their Home

During the measure is another opportunity to create reciprocity. Ask if you can measure and inspect all the areas of flooring, not just the sections you are replacing. Ask to inspect their vacuum and walk-off mats, and to see what kind of carpet spotter they are using. After you finish, write out a customized maintenance plan on how to maintain not only the floors they are purchasing from you, but the flooring they aren't having you replace. This creates even more feelings of reciprocity.

Testimonials

No matter how good you are at describing your products and services, it will always sound 100 times more convincing coming from someone else, even if you are 100 times more eloquent.

Testimonials are a single element that will dramatically increase the response of just about any marketing campaign or strategy. Websites, Direct Response letters, display ads, newspaper inserts, flyers, newsletters, backs of business cards, CD's, DVD's ... anything.

You should always educate your prospects about the benefits of doing business with you versus your competitors. But no matter how good you are at explaining the benefits to your prospects, it will always sound 100 times more convincing coming from someone else. Why? Because it's not *you* saying it. This is called the "Halo Effect." When someone else sings your praises (instead of you) it automatically gives you a halo of credibility. Therefore, you should always use testimonials in your marketing whenever possible.

Stop Using Meaningless, Copycat Slogans

What The...?!

Your customers have seen thousands of advertising messages from businesses, all claiming they are the best, number one in customer satisfaction, highest quality, longest lasting, blah, blah, blah. They are NUMB to these kinds of claims. They don't even hear them anymore. Claims of "we're the best" float through their craniums unnoticed.

Yet the majority of floor dealers continue using these dried out, me-too, boring, copycat slogans.

Don't be like the majority! Shun meaningless slogans like they were advertisement lepers. *(Unclean!)*

Instead, use strong USP's, including testimonials.

How to use testimonials

Written testimonials. Testimonial portfolio. Marketing letters. The back of your business card. Newsletters. Basically you want to use them everywhere. I can't think of a single marketing strategy that can't be improved with testimonials.

Testimonial portfolio. As you collect testimonials, assemble them into a nice, three-ring binder using sheet protectors. Make photocopies of thank you cards and letters. Keep the portfolio in your "design room," or wherever you do your customer consultations.

Brag wall. A place to hang dozens of testimonials where walk-in customers will see them.

Audio testimonials. Use them while customers are on hold in your phone system. Compile them onto an audio CD and give them to prospects.

Video testimonials. Use them on your website. Edit several of them together into a DVD. You don't want it to look too slick. It should look like a home video of your kid's birthday party. If you make it too slick people will think you hired actors.

Education-Based Marketing

People who are interested in floor covering are craving information. They have no idea how to choose one store over another, which product to choose, etc. All too often this means that they wind up choosing by the worst possible criteria: *price*. Savvy dealers I coach always make sure that *they* are the ones to arm prospects with the information they need to choose wisely: in other words, to choose *their* dealership instead of their competitor's! And one tool they use to accomplish this is a done-for-them consumer's guide I created, which they give to all their prospects.

You should do the same: Create a consumer's guide or a free report and give it to anyone who visits or calls your business. This is important for five reasons:

1.   It positions you as an expert.

2.   It gives you a chance to educate your prospects on the benefits of your dealership.

3.   It helps your prospects make a well-informed decision on which dealership and which products to choose. (Your dealership and your products, of course!)

4.   It differentiates you from the competition. After all, how many other dealers give out consumer guides?

5.   It creates value in the mind of your prospect.

How To Create Your Consumer's Guide

Consumer's guides, free reports, white papers: You've probably heard of these before, and they all mean basically the same thing. They are a means of educating consumers on a topic in your industry.

The best way to explain how to create a consumer's guide is to deconstruct the guide I created for dealers. To write this report, I did the following:

- **Common misconceptions.** I identified misconceptions that consumers have about buying flooring. For example, one misconception is that price is all that matters. I went into great detail explaining why cheap price and high quality never go together. That flooring is the most important part of your interior design, and you want it to not only look great, but last a long time.

- **Consumer warnings.** I educate consumers on a number of common industry rip-offs to look out for. For example, I explain that while box stores and online dealers may offer warranties, getting them to honor a warranty is a different story. I explain that one way they charge dirt-cheap prices is by offering warranties, but then delaying and giving customers the runaround if they need to make a warranty claim.

- **Common mistakes to avoid.** The guide contains six mistakes to avoid when choosing a dealer. For example, I detail why it's a huge mistake to buy flooring from an online dealer with no physical presence in their area.

- **Questions to ask a dealer.** In the guide I give five questions to ask a dealer before purchasing. I tell them that if a dealer can't answer "yes" to all five, to buy from someone else. For example, "Do you have written testimonials?" Most dealers don't. But the dealer using this guide has been trained to use testimonials, so he can say "yes." The other questions are also "stacked" to favor the dealer using the guide.

Using these bullets as a template, you can create your own consumer's guide or free report.

How To Use Your Consumer's Guide

Every walk-in should be given a copy of your guide. These are also good follow-up for people who call your store but don't come in right away. Get their name and address and send them your report. Say something like, "I understand that you're shopping for flooring right now. I offer a booklet called *How To Choose A Floor Dealer*. In it you'll learn how to avoid predatory dealers, seven costly misconceptions about floor covering, and six mistakes to avoid when choosing a floor covering store. What's your mailing address so I can send you a copy?"

(Hint: Notice I didn't say, "Can I send you a copy?" That gives them the option to say "no." Instead, I asked for their mailing address. I didn't even give them the option to say "no.")

Now you will have their name and address, so you can send them your welcome pack, and other marketing materials. You can also follow up with them and ask them what they liked about the report, and get them to visit your store.

Zero-Resistance Strategies (11 of 33)

1. Market to your sphere of influence, beginning with your past customers. Use a monthly *Direct Response Newsletter*.

2. Market to your employees' and sales team's sphere of influence.

3. Have a *Sales Closer System* in place.

4. Have a *Referral Marketing System* in place.

5. Use testimonials in all your marketing, in your showroom, and during your *Sales Closer System*.

6. Use consumer education (free report or consumer's guide).

7. Promote your USP in all your marketing, in your showroom, and during your *Sales Closer System*.

8. Use your guarantees and warranties as USP's.

9. Bake fresh cookies or bread in your store. Keep the baked goods up front and offer them to walk-ins. (The aroma feels inviting, puts customers at ease, and it creates differentiation.)

10. Have a beverage bar. Hand walk-ins a beverage menu and ask them what they'd like to drink.

11. Everyone on staff wears uniforms. (Slacks, dress shoes, and a polo shirt with the company logo is fine.)

CASE STUDY

How Customer Education Helps Sam Close More Sales At Higher Prices

Sam Quandahl is the owner of Floor Coverings of Winona in Minnesota. He has made customer education a part of his sales process by using a consumer's guide that I created for my floor dealers.

Along with the consumer guide, Sam has also implemented the *Design Audit* sales closer system. He told me, "*The Design Audit* has proven to be a power-ful sales tool that quickly positions me and my sales team as Trusted Advisors, and totally separates us from the other dealers. Since we began using these two strategies, response from customers has been tremendous, and our closed-sale batting average has gone way up."

237

His sales team is also excited about these tools. One day one of them excitedly pulled him aside and told him that some "skeptical shoppers" came into the store to buy flooring. When they left—without buying—she gave them the consumer's guide. A few days later the couple came back and told her that they had shopped at several other stores, but were going to buy from Floor Coverings of Winona. This in spite of the fact that Floor Coverings of Winona is more expensive than most of the other dealers. They told her that a big part of their decision was because of the impression the consumer's guide had made on them.

And it gets even better. The customers told the salesperson, "It says in the guide that we get a free *Design Audit*." You see, because the guide educated the customers on the value of the sales process, they were eager to participate. With traditional advertising, this kind of attitude from prospects about a "sales process" is very rare. Typically they look upon a "sales process" and root canal surgery with about the same level of enthusiasm. But in this case they *wanted* the sales process, and went out of their way to request it. This demonstrates the power of consumer education.

During the visit, the salesperson asked the customers what she could do to exceed their expectations. Their reply: "You already have!" They then immediately scheduled an appointment to have their house measured. No hesitation. No needing to "think about it." When Sam was through measuring they demanded that he take a check, even though they hadn't decided on the final color.

Another female customer commented to Sam: "As we were reading through the consumer's guide, it really made us feel that you want to know what we need and what will really help us. It made it very personable." She also bought from Sam rather than his lower-priced competitors.

Consumer education is a highly effective method to combat the ever-growing skepticism, distrust, and price sensitivity among consumers. Therefore, it needs to be part of your overall marketing strategy if you want to maximize your success in the 21st century. It completely changes the perception your prospects and customers have of you. By educating your prospects and customers, they see you as a Trusted Advisor, someone they can rely on to give them professional recommendations. The dealer who successfully implements this strategy gives him or herself an instant advantage over competitors. But by not implementing consumer education, you place yourself at risk of losing sales to a dealer down the street who has implemented it. Just like Sam's competitors are losing sales to *him*.

....

SEVENTEEN

HOW TO HANDLE TOXIC CUSTOMERS

FLOOR DEALER: Today was rough. I spent over an hour with a lady who was rude, demanding, and treated me like a criminal.

JIM: Why did you give her permission to do that?

WARNING: This chapter doesn't pull any punches, and contains opinions and language that some may consider harsh and/or offensive. Read at your own risk.

The 60-something-year-old lady who answered the door was extremely sweet and invited me right into her lovely home. I was there because she was interested in hiring my company to clean her carpets. This was back in 1998 or so, and I'd only been in business a short time. I was good at sales, but still a little green in some other areas.

I began measuring and inspecting her floors, and everything started out very pleasantly. Then her husband walked in. This guy had a chip on his shoulder the size of a small water buffalo, and he immediately went to work on me. He interrogated me on my pricing, wondered loudly why I was asking so many questions about the carpet, and generally made it very clear that he thought I was trying to steal him blind, and that he didn't trust me (or anyone else). The man was so rude that several times his wife said, "Charlie, *please!*"

I felt genuinely sorry for the poor lady having to live with such a complete ass.

Anyway, I was so intent on "overcoming objections" and "closing the sale" that I allowed this guy to follow me around and abuse me for the entire 40 minutes I was there. When I finally handed him the quote for the various cleaning packages, he made it very clear that my prices were so high as to be "offensive." "Holy shit!" he blurted, "When do you plan to retire?"

"Just as soon as I finish cleaning your carpets," I calmly replied.

I didn't get the job.

Jim's Tail Between The Legs Policy

Looking back I blush thinking about how I permitted myself to be abused. The one good thing that came out of this experience, and a few others like it, was that I began to make internal, personal changes so this would never happen again. I decided that I did not deserve to be treated this way; that I would always treat my customers with the utmost respect, but I would also demand the same in return.

Thus *Jim's Tail Between The Legs Policy* was born. It goes like this: *I will treat customers with respect, but if a customer decides not to reciprocate, if they are bound and determined that one of us is going to leave our encounter with their tail between their legs, it's going to be them, not me.*

I was on the phone a while back with the customer service department of a company with which I was doing an important, time-sensitive financial transaction. They were supposed to have sent some essential paperwork to me via email, and one of their staff was supposed to have phoned me. Neither happened. I asked the fellow on the other end of the line (I'll call him Anthony) why I had gotten no response. He said that the items were emailed, and that they had tried to call me. I asked him what email address and phone number they had for me, and when he read them back they were both completely wrong; not even close. So I gave him my correct email address and asked him to spell it back, letter by letter to make sure he had it right. He snickered into the phone, and then read it back to me in a condescending tone, but not letter for letter; he just read the words in the address. I again asked him to please read it letter by letter. He obviously thought I was being anal, and continued his condescending tone, snickering into the phone again.

I'd had enough.

"Look, Anthony!" I barked, "I don't want to hear your obnoxious little laughs. You guys were supposed to have had that paperwork to me weeks ago, but you screwed up not only my email address, but my phone number. You're going to make sure you've got both of them correct in your system, and you're going to spell my email address back to me letter-for-letter."

He immediately backed down, took on an extremely contrite tone, and read back my email address, which was academic at this point because I'll never, ever, ever do business with this company again.

Anthony had decided to try to make me feel foolish (i.e., tuck my tail between my legs), but that goes against my policy. Since *he* created a situation where one of us was going to tuck tail, I made sure it was *him*. That's my policy.

The entrepreneurial game is 90% mental.

How many times has a price-sensitive, tire-kicking, price-shopping, suspicious-of-everyone, pain-in-the-ass, bottom feeder walked into your store and put you through the wringer, thus ruining your morning?

In my early days in business, back in my 20's, I had days where my ability to function was literally wiped out by one, solitary, small-minded, toxic jerk. My productivity dropped to near zero. Essentially I gave permission to a toxic person to invade my life and steal my time (time is money) and peace of mind. And here's the kicker: *This person couldn't have done it without my permission.* Why in the name of all that's righteous and holy was I giving these peons permission to screw up my day?

Never again.

One thing that's important to keep in mind is that you never, ever, ever want to do business with a toxic person. Once you discover that someone is toxic, immediately cease all interaction with them. Stop trying to overcome objections, stop trying to "sell" them, work with them, etc. You can do this in such a way that you preserve your dignity and your peace of mind. To do this, I think it's important to remember this famous verse from the Bible:

Do not throw your pearls before swine, or they will trample them under their feet, and turn and tear you to pieces. Matthew 7:6

243

Let's say someone walks into your store and immediately begins to exhibit signs of toxicity. Your conversation might go something like this:

YOU: Welcome to Jimbo's Floors. Are you a new or returning customer?

TOXIC JERK: New customer.

YOU: Great! We have a program for new customers. Can I take a quick minute and tell you about it?

TOXIC JERK: No. I just want to know the price on some carpeting for my house.

YOU: O.K. How many people live at your house? What's the level of traffic like?

TOXIC JERK: (Impatiently, like you're really putting a kink in her day.) It's just me and my husband.

YOU: Do you own any pets?

TOXIC JERK: (Huffs and sighs.) I have one dog. Look, I know what kind of carpet I want, and right now I'm just getting prices.

YOU: Fair enough. On what are you going to base your final decision?

TOXIC JERK: Well ... whoever has the best price.

YOU: By "best price" do you mean the cheapest?

TOXIC JERK: Well … yes.

YOU: Oh, I'm glad you said that because I can save us both a lot of wasted time. You see, we're the most expensive in town. (Then shut up. First one to talk loses. You've just taken away her only weapon. She's most likely never encountered someone with the cojones to say this to her. Let 'er squirm.)

TOXIC JERK: Well … uh … can't you just give me a price?

YOU: We cater to customers who are interested in quality, not cheapest price. If you're looking for the cheapest I can tell you right now that we are not the right company for you. (Then shut up and listen. First one to talk loses.)

I've actually had people change their tune at this point and I wind up getting them as customers. However, at this point she will most likely either leave or continue to try and get a price out of you. Stand your ground. For example:

TOXIC JERK: Well, I'm interested in quality *and* a good price.

YOU: Which are you more interested in? Quality or cheap price? Because you can't have both. (Then shut up.)

She's also most likely never met a floor dealer — or any salesperson — with the cojones to tell her she can't have something. She's used to everyone kow-towing. This will rock her world. You'll also notice that when she says "good" or "best" price, I keep changing it to "cheap." The word "cheap" has very negative connotations and your use of it implies that she is cheap, and will drive the dagger home. I've actually had customers get angry with me when I stand my ground and refuse to give them a price. This just makes things more fun for me. See, when you adopt the "tail between the legs policy,"

245

dealing with the occasional toxic customer becomes fun and it makes for a great water-cooler story.

However, if you cave in and give a price at this point, you have just cast your pearls before a swine and she will turn and tear you to pieces by complaining about the price, or simply leaving and never coming back. Don't give her the satisfaction or allow your peace of mind to be robbed in this fashion.

Now, if she absolutely, positively seems to be changing her tune (like I said, it happens sometimes), then make her promise not to price shop you. Say something like this:

YOU: O.K., if I agree to work with you, I'm going to take you through a full consultation just like I do for all my customers, and then we'll schedule an in-home visit, and that's when I'll give you exact quotes on several grades of flooring to help you find something that fits your budget and lifestyle. Now, if I invest the time to do all this, and I'm able to give you a solution that fits your budget, are you going to buy from us or keep shopping?

In other words, the tables are now turned. It's no longer you trying to sell her flooring; she now has to sell you on allowing her to be a customer. If you sense any hesitation whatsoever at this point, send her packing. If she agrees, then make her go through the consultation, look at your testimonials, schedule an in-home visit, the whole bit. When you give her the quote, build in a secret 10% pain-in-the-ass fee.

Whether she buys or turns around and leaves, it doesn't matter. You have preserved your integrity and peace of mind; you haven't cast your pearls before swine. If she leaves without buying, *she's* the one with her tail between her legs, not you.

Jimmy Tells Price Shoppers That He's The Most Expensive ... And Still Gets The Sale!

Jimmy Williams owns Factory Flooring and Design in North Carolina, and has been in business for over 40 years.

Like most dealers, he occasionally has people try to beat him up on price. But he uses one of my "tail between the legs" strategies to instantly turn the tables on them.

"I had a fellow come into the store, trying to beat me up on price," Jimmy told me. "I decided to use the strategy you talk about in your program. I looked him in the eye and told him that we're the highest priced store in the county, and that I'm sorry, but we probably wouldn't be able to help him. I handed him my card, and as I turned away he said, 'But wait ...'"

He bought. At *Jimmy's* price.

This happened twice within a couple of weeks of my conversation with Jimmy. For most dealers, the thought of telling a prospect that they're the most expensive strikes terror in their hearts. But by using the zero-resistance sales strategies in this book, and the principles outlined in this chapter—not to mention some good old fashioned guts—Jimmy is not only able to command premium prices, but look price shoppers in the face and tell them he's the most expensive store in the county. And he lands many of those sales. He also instantly snatches away the price shopper's biggest weapon. If they say he's too expensive, he says, "Yup, we're the most expensive in town. We're probably not the right store for you."

BOOM!

What else is the prospect going to say? He's just fired his biggest gun and the bullet bounced off Jimmy's chest.

And it gets even better. By first telling the prospect that he's the most expensive, and then following it up with "We probably won't be able to help you," Jimmy is subtly letting the prospect know that if he doesn't buy from him, he's proving that he's a cheapskate. Jimmy has turned the prospect's implied insult that "you're not worth the price you're asking" right back on him. Brilliant!

How would it feel to be able to do the same thing with prospects who try to beat *you* up on price? Empowering? Fun? Exhilarating? Liberating? Yup. I've done this in my businesses, and the feeling is amazing. The strategies in this book can empower you to do the same. You've just got to implement them. The choice is yours.

EIGHTEEN

....

THIRTEEN DEADLY
MARKETING MISTAKES

FLOOR DEALER: My advertising results are really lousy.

JIM: Who are you targeting your message to?

FLOOR DEALER: Targeting?

How To Avoid A Slow, Painful Death

Once upon a time flooring dealers could expect seasonal surges in business at predictable times each year. They could also count on a certain amount of repeat and referral business to happen "automatically." All of this has changed. With the explosion of box stores and online discounters, and with the proliferation of 24-hour news outlets (which can quickly erode consumer confidence with an unexpected surge of "bad" news), dealers can't count on anything to happen automatically anymore. At best, relying on traditional methods for getting customers—methods that may have once worked—will hurt a dealer's ability to thrive and grow. At worst, it will mean a slow, painful death of their business.

This chapter focuses on how to avoid many of the deadly marketing mistakes that can kill a dealership, and instead turn them into strategies that will give you an *Unfair Advantage* over competitors, and help you beat the boxes.

Mistake #1: Failing to promote your unique selling proposition (USP)

Most dealers try to be all things to all people, and consequently they wind up using generic descriptions of their business. Look at any floor covering ad and you will likely see one of the following adjectives or phrases: *Trusted, Friendly, Professional, Free Quotes, Best Value, 100% Satisfaction.* These mean absolutely nothing to the consumer because they convey no clear, compelling benefit. They also have zero impact because *everybody* says it!

Compare the examples above with FedEx's unique selling proposition: *When it absolutely, positively has to be there overnight.* This gives a specific, clear, easily understood benefit to the customer. It focuses like a laser beam, and gives the customer an obvious reason to use FedEx instead of all the other mailing services.

Ask yourself this question: *Why should my prospect choose my business versus any/every other floor dealer available to them?* Once you come up with a clear, compelling answer to that question, you'll have your USP.

Mistake #2: Having no target market

There's a marketing saying that goes: "If everyone is your customer, no one is your customer." A gigantic mistake made by the majority of dealers is trying to be all things to all people. This leads to two problems:

First, in an attempt to reach "everyone" with their advertising, they cast a net so wide and so broad that it's impossible to get any market penetration. It's very, very expensive and time consuming to attempt market penetration for every single person in a geographical market area. Most dealers simply don't have the deep pockets necessary to duplicate the "brand name building" done by corporations like Home Depot, Lowe's, and Empire.

Second, in an attempt to speak to "everybody" they are forced to water down their advertising message. Instead of crafting a benefit-laden message aimed at a carefully chosen audience, they wind up using mass media (newspaper, television, and radio) to spread meaningless clichés like those mentioned above. This is horribly inefficient, and small business owners simply can't afford the luxury of this kind of waste. Most flooring dealers who succeed do so *in spite of*, rather than *because of*, this kind of advertising.

By identifying your market—your ideal customer who desires your services and will pay your prices regardless of what the competitors charge—you are then able to build a message that speaks directly to them, then use media to deliver that message with pin-point accuracy. This follows the formula of Message, Market, and Media that I discussed earlier.

Mistake #3: Being dishonest, unethical, or misleading

Odds are if you care enough about your business to be reading this book, you're probably not a sleazy, bait-n-switch type of dealer. So this is more of an encouragement for you to keep fighting the good fight when it comes to being ethical.

In the short term, you can make money ripping people off. It's a fact. It gets done all the time. But there are huge tradeoffs: your peace of mind (trying to remember which lie you told to whom), longevity in the business, your reputation, and your sanity. When you're scamming people, it's simply not possible to have a long-term, joyful business, or to look at yourself each morning in the mirror and feel good about what you see. Yes, by being honest you may have to re-order cushion when they deliver a lower grade than your customer requested (instead of just installing it … who would know, right?). But in the long run, by remaining ethical even when it hurts a little, you give yourself the foundation for longevity, profitability, and peace of mind that the sleaze-balls will never enjoy.

Mistake #4: Focusing on features instead of benefits

The three words you need to remember when creating a marketing message are: benefits, benefits, benefits. When it comes to your product or service, the only thing your customers and potential customers care about is how they can benefit. Period. Yet too often sales and marketing efforts by dealers focus on features: certified installers, stain resistant carpet, cushion thickness, etc. Yes, these features are beneficial to the customer, but in your sales and marketing you need to spell out exactly how the customer will benefit from a trained installer, higher yarn counts, and stain resistant carpet. Don't expect them to connect the dots; do it for them.

Mistake #5: Not marketing to your past customers

This is huge. If you are making this mistake, you'll leave millions of dollars over the course of your career on the table. In fact, out of the 13 mistakes this one is the biggest.

Most dealers spend the majority of their time, energy, and money slugging it out in the market place to get a new customer while totally ignoring the only people in the known universe who have proven that they will do business with them: their past customers. This is utterly INSANE!

Let me bottom-line it for you: Your customers need to hear from you a minimum of 12 times per year with entertaining, informative, value-added communication if you are to have any hope of cutting through the advertising clutter they are bombarded with each and every day. This is best accomplished with a Direct Response Newsletter. This strategy has enabled my dealers to develop businesses that are 80%-100% repeat and referral driven, thus dramatically lowering their marketing costs and at the same time raising the quality of customer.

Mistake #6: Failure to have a *Referral Marketing System*

Any dealer that does a decent job servicing their customers will eventually begin to generate referrals. However, for most dealers, referrals are at best a happy accident; a bonus. If you're serious about thriving in any market, you need to have a system in place that actively farms your past and current customers for referrals. Here's why this is so powerful: Let's say that you have a very small database of 1,000 customers. Even if those customers are extremely loyal, there is a good chance that in any given month only a handful of them need your services. However, each one of them has a sphere of influence of at least 200 others. That's 200,000 potential customers, and each month a truckload of that larger group will need your services! By having a system in place that taps in to your customer's sphere for referrals, you expand your market exponentially. The *Core 3* strategies are highly effective for making this happen.

Mistake #7: Never testing new marketing methods in Tiers 2 and 3

There can be severe negative consequences for relying too heavily on a single Tier 2 or Tier 3 strategy. What happens if that strategy suddenly stops working? Back in the 1990's there was a period where I was generating 30% of all new customers from a single sales letter, and it worked well for two years. Suddenly it stopped working. Fortunately I had several other strategies in place, including my Tier 1 strategies, but initially I lost one-third of my revenue from new customers and it caused a real cash-crunch as I struggled to replace it. It's better to have 10 different Tier 2 and Tier 3 strategies each producing one new customer, than just one strategy producing 10 customers.

Mistake #8: Expecting your ads to give the entire marketing message

Ad space is very expensive, and buying space large enough to present your entire marketing message is cost prohibitive and unnecessary. It's possible to use relatively small ad space to offer your free report or consumer's guide, which will in turn give a complete marketing message. For example, here's a small classified ad that will work on Craigslist or a printed publication:

```
Shopping For Flooring? WARNING: Don't call or visit
any floor dealer until you get this FREE report, How
To Choose A Flooring Dealer. You will learn 6 cost-
ly mistakes to avoid, 7 common misconceptions about
flooring, and 3 dirty little secrets about installa-
tions that many dealers hope you never find out. For
instant access visit www.YourURLHere.com.
```

Mistake #9: Assuming your customers understand floor covering

As a professional flooring dealer who eats, sleeps, breathes, and drinks flooring each and every day, it's easy to forget that your customers and prospects don't understand flooring. This leads to several problems. First, dealers and salespeople talk about features instead of benefits to the customer. It's critical that in your sales and marketing efforts you connect the dots for your customers as to how they will benefit from the positive features of your products and services. Second, because dealers assume their customers understand flooring, they ignore the tremendous power of education-based marketing. By educating your customers, you help them understand why quality and low price never go together and why they should invest in one type of flooring versus another. Educating your customers also positions you as a Trusted Advisor; like a family doctor to be trusted rather than as a "salesperson" trying to hock your wares.

My dealers and I have used education-based marketing as part of our overall marketing mixes for years with tremendous results. Don't underestimate the benefits of educating your customers.

Mistake #10: Failing to position yourself as a Trusted Advisor

I want you to get a picture in your mind of a family doctor in his white coat with clipboard and stethoscope; he is mild-mannered and cares about your well-being. Are you picturing it? Good. Now, next to that image I want you to picture a used car salesman who will do anything to "make a deal." Are you seeing those two pictures in your mind? Now ask yourself this: *Who do I trust more?* Unless you've pictured an extraordinarily sleazy family doctor, he is obviously the one you will tend to trust. This is because you know a doctor is looking out for your best interest. He is a Trusted Advisor that you seek out for his advice and expertise. That's how you want your customers to picture you. Two powerful strategies for doing this are using testimonials and customer education. First, you will probably recall my saying this: What others say about you is 100 times more effective than what you say about yourself, even if you're 100 times more eloquent. So use the power of testimonials! Second, use customer education. By educating your customers, you position yourself as the trusted expert in your field.

Mistake #11: Failing to market to customers who are "hot"

Buying flooring is an exciting event for your customers. They think about it, dream about it, talk about it, and then think about it some more. It's important to have a marketing plan in place to "farm" these "hot" customers for referrals and additional business. At no other time in your relationship with them will you have an opportunity where they are so predisposed to give you referrals. In the *Core 3* Referral Marketing chapter I outline a highly effective, proven strategy for capitalizing on this "hot" period.

The Reticular Activator

Another effective strategy I teach dealers for capitalizing on the "hot" period is the Reticular Activator (RA) campaign. You may be asking, "What the heck is a reticular activator?" It's a psychological condition where your mind begins to notice very specific things. Pregnant women notice other pregnant women. If you just bought a white Ford Explorer, you'll tend to notice other white SUV's. If you buy a pair of blue Nike cross-trainers you'll notice other blue Nike cross-trainers. That's your reticular activator. Well, the same thing happens when people are in the process of buying flooring. They notice the kinds of flooring they are walking on, they notice ads about flooring, and they bring it up in conversation and notice if someone else brings it up. The RA campaign takes advantage of this. It works like this:

- Once a customer puts down their deposit, the dealer sends them weekly printed mailers that congratulate them on their decision, and remind them of the dealer's referral program. This continues for four weeks, or until the installation is complete, whichever comes first.

- The dealer also sends out emails every few days that reinforce this message.

- These mailers are super fun and entertaining, and very different from what the customer will have ever seen from a floor dealer. For example, one letter has a dollar bill stapled to the top and talks about how the customer will be rewarded for their referrals.

A system like this helps my dealers turn one sale into multiple sales with extremely low marketing costs. You should do the same.

Mistake #12: Failing to market continuously

A scuba diver can forget to breathe regularly. In order to remember to breathe, scuba divers are taught to think of ABC—*Always Breath Continuously*. In marketing, flooring dealers need to think of AMC—*Always Market Continuously*. Marketing is the oxygen that your business breathes in order to survive. Don't cut off your business's oxygen supply. Always have strategies in place that are getting the phone to ring and customers coming in your door. It's easy to get complacent when you have a lot of business. The Great Recession taught dealers that this can change in a very short time. It's critical to have marketing systems in place that will produce a constant influx of new business.

Mistake #13: Failing to use testimonials

Testimonials are a single element that will dramatically increase the response of just about any marketing campaign or strategy. It's important to educate your prospects about the wonderful benefits of doing business with you. But no matter how eloquent you are at explaining the benefits to your prospects, it will always sound 100 times more convincing coming from someone else. Your customers have seen thousands of advertising messages from businesses, all claiming they are the best, number one in customer satisfaction, highest quality, longest lasting, ad infinitum, ad nausea. They are NUMB to these kinds of claims. They don't even hear them anymore. Claims of "We're the best" float through their craniums unnoticed. Testimonials are the *key* for cutting through what they perceive to be mere hype.

NINETEEN

....

THE SYSTEM-DEPENDENT FLOORING DEALERSHIP

FLOOR DEALER: You can't find good help these days.

JIM: Do you have *written*, step-by-step systems in place so your new employees and sales people know exactly what's expected of them? And do you train them on the system? And do you hold them accountable to follow the system as trained?

FLOOR DEALER: No.

JIM: Then your problem isn't *finding* good help. It's equipping good help once it's found.

Why Dealers Are Slaves To Their Stores

If you walk into a McDonald's, you won't see the owner in the back flipping burgers, making French fries, or taking orders. You won't see him wiping down tables, taking out the trash, or mopping the dining area. In fact, you probably won't even *see* the owner because he is out playing golf, traveling, or working on his other business ventures. Yet the business continues to operate smoothly and churn out profits for the owner. This happens in spite of the fact that a McDonald's franchise is essentially a complex manufacturing plant using hormone-raging teenagers as its work force.

However, walk into a typical floor dealership and you'll see the owner wearing 20 different hats, putting out fires, working 50-70 hours per week, stressed out, burned out, and wondering where he went wrong in life. He has to be physically present at his business or things quickly start falling through the cracks. If he were to leave for an extended absence, say a month, he would likely return to a business in shambles. This happens in spite of the fact that he is using (supposedly) mature, professional adults with lots of experience as his work force.

What's the difference? It's very simple. The McDonald's is *system*-dependent while the typical floor dealership is *owner*-dependent.

The Franchise Model

The typical career path for a floor dealer goes something like this:

He starts out as an installer (or working in the family business), and eventually thinks, "Hey, I know a lot about flooring. Why don't I start my own business?" So he hangs out his shingle. He soon finds himself working more and more hours, far more than he ever did as an installer or an employee. His stress level goes through the roof, his personal life goes by the wayside, and he's left wondering if going into business for himself wasn't the biggest mistake of his life! Sitting in his office trying to catch up on paperwork at the end of another 12-hour day, he reminisces about the good old days of being an employee. Why wouldn't he? His employees left hours ago and are at home with their families. Some of them might even be making more money than he does!

So what went wrong? This in a nutshell: He mistakenly believed that the skills he had as a flooring *technician* were the same skills required to run a successful flooring *business*. This is a gigantic myth that has caused the failure of more flooring stores than any other single cause. It's why four out of five small businesses across all industry categories fail in the first few years of their existence.

Tackling this technician/business-owner misconception is the topic of *The E-Myth* by Michael Gerber. (*E* stands for *entrepreneurial*.) In his book, Gerber says that the solution to the E-Myth is this: A business owner should build his business as though he were going to franchise it even if he never does. Doing this has a number of benefits:

- Allows the owner to work *on* his business rather than *in* his business
- Greater profitability
- Unlimited ability to expand
- The power to begin other business ventures
- The ability to have a rewarding, fulfilling life outside of the business
- Early retirement, or the option to retire early
- Business can be sold at a premium

Engineering your flooring business so that it's set up to sell is powerful because you not only are able to reap all the benefits listed above, but you now have the ability to sell if you need or want to. Also, with your business set up like a franchise, the buyer doesn't necessarily need to have a background in flooring. This opens up a whole new pool of investors.

Many dealers think that because their business is doing $1.2 million per year that their business is worth $1.2 million, or some multiple of it. When it comes time to sell they are often stunned to find that locating an interested buyer is very difficult, and that no one wants to pay them much more for their business than the value of the inventory and equipment. The reason this happens is because many dealers don't own a business; they own a *job*. Investors want to buy investments, not jobs. So if you're interested in ever selling your business, then you need to look at it from an investor's point of view. They aren't eager to invest in a business where they have to work 60-70 hours per week just to keep it running. They want a business that churns out profits without the need for them to be physically present constantly. You should want the same thing.

How do you make this happen? You engineer your business so it's system-dependent, like the McDonald's franchise. And that begins with your mindset.

Realize Who You Are

Your job description is not any of the day-to-day tasks that are done in your business. You may be performing some of these jobs—like selling, installing, bookkeeping, ordering products, etc.—but that is not your primary function.

Here is what you are: a rancher. A herder. A marketer of flooring services. This is a subtle distinction, but an important one. Think of your business as a ship. On board your ship are all kinds of jobs that need to be done to keep your ship moving.

- Bookkeeper
- Receptionist
- Installer
- Office manager
- Sales

As the business owner, you are the captain of the ship. You are the visionary who decides where your ship will go, and how fast it will get there. Even though you are the captain, I realize that your business may be small right now, and so you may be performing some of the jobs on your ship like bookkeeping, answering phones, and selling. You might even be handling *all* of the jobs. But as a business owner, your job description is *not* those jobs. This is a concept that many dealers miss. Once you begin to see yourself as the owner of a business, you approach the building of your business from a completely different standpoint.

- You begin to see jobs as items to eventually be delegated, not as tasks for *you* to shoulder.

- You begin to think in terms of making a profit, not just making a living.

- You begin to build your business around your life, instead of your life around your business.

I am not saying that you should stop doing a function that you truly love. If you like to sell, keep doing it. But here is something to think about. What would it be worth to you to have the following list of items active in your business?

- Be at the store only when you want

- Never worry about answering phones, paying the bills, and most of the other administrative "stuff" that goes into running a store

- Never feel the need to deal with difficult customers you would rather not because you need the money

- Focus on doing what you love most in life, what you are best at

Think your stress level would go down? Think you would enjoy your business more? Maybe be a more effective entrepreneur? Maybe enjoy *life* a little more?

Use Systems To Give Your Customers A Consistent, Quality Experience

Years ago there was a lube shop where I used to take my car. This place looked very sharp from the outside. It was clean with neat landscaping, and the exterior paint job was bright and cheerful. The color scheme tied in with their uniforms and brochures. Every single time I visited (and I mean *every* time) they did the following:

- The technicians were all clean-cut and wearing a uniform (no grease monkeys).

- They greeted me, showed me where to park, and asked how they could be of service.

- They called me sir or Mr. Armstrong and were consistently polite.

- They used my license plate number to pull up my entire service history. (They didn't have to ask for my name, telephone number, or anything.)

- They invited me to sit in their CLEAN waiting area.

- They always had current issues of six or eight popular magazines, and that day's edition of the local paper.

- They provided fresh, hot coffee in a CLEAN serving area, plus nice vending machines with snacks and sodas.

- They performed a 29-point checkup on my car.

- While I waited, the technician who worked on my car came into the waiting area, knelt next to my chair, and politely recommended other minor repairs that my car needed (belts, wipers, transmission service, etc.).

- Everyone was serviced in turn. While I waited, others who were ahead of me were politely called to the counter when their vehicles were ready.

- They vacuumed my car for free.

- When they finished, they politely called me to the counter and went over the bill with me in a very organized and professional manner.

- My car was parked outside the waiting area ready to roll with the keys in the ignition.

- All the technicians I passed on the way to my car waved and told me to have a nice day.

The whole experience was more like visiting a well-run doctor's office than a lube shop. Well, these folks did not provide smog checks, and one weekend I needed to get my car smogged, so I went to another shop. While I was there I asked them to go ahead and change the oil. This shop was also clean and sharp looking on the outside. The exterior paint job had a nice theme and was very cheerful. However, while this shop provided many of the services of my regular shop, here is what they didn't do:

- The technicians were not clean-cut, and did not wear uniforms. The cashier was wearing a halter top.

- No one greeted me. I had to look for a place to park.

- No one called me sir or Mr. Armstrong, or even used my first name.

- The waiting area was not very clean.

- All the magazines were old and many were tattered. No newspaper.

- There was no 29-point checkup.

- No one suggested repairs. In fact, after the smog check, they forgot the oil change and I had to remind them.

- They didn't vacuum my car.

- My car sat outside ready to go for 10 minutes before they called me to the counter. This was due to a fairly disorganized system (or no system) for processing their customers.

- My keys were left sitting on the counter. The cashier asked me, "Are these your keys?" They were not organized.

- Each customer was dealt with in a different manner. People would accidentally be serviced in front of others who had been waiting longer. There were no routines to keep things organized.

- Nobody waved or said have a nice day as I walked to my car.

The people at this shop were very friendly, I wasn't treated rudely, and they did a perfectly good job servicing my vehicle. This shop was a lot closer to my home, and the oil change was about $2 less than where I usually went. But I never used them again for an oil change. Why? Among other things, I realized that every time I visited them I'd never know what to expect. I knew that they had no routine for servicing customers so I couldn't expect a quality experience each time. I also didn't feel good about the experience. When I left my regular lube shop, I always went away feeling like I was well taken care of; that these people cared enough about my patronage to keep things organized, efficient, and friendly. I was a valued guest and they did things to make me want to come back.

Not so with the other shop. I didn't exactly feel *bad* when I left. I just didn't feel valued. I didn't get the impression that they cared very much whether or not I came back. Oh, I'm sure they wanted me back, but they didn't put out much effort to demonstrate this.

Now, you may think I am being overly critical of the second shop, that I really nit-picked them, that I was unfair. Well, here's some real-world information for you: Any potential customer who values good service over low price, every customer who is not a price shopper will be just as ruthless. People do not pay premium prices for organizational problems. The only hope for this second shop is to offer prices so low that people will tolerate mediocre service. But their prices are already so low that this will be very difficult to do and remain profitable.

Go back and compare both lists that I made of the services I received from both shops. How hard would it be for the second shop to make corrections and operate at the same level, or higher, than the first shop? Not hard at all. How much would it cost? Very little. In fact, the biggest expense would probably be for uniforms and a little additional training. But in reality, it wouldn't cost them one thin dime. It would make them thousands of extra dollars because they could charge higher prices, and they would keep their customers. They would have kept me.

We're talking some very simple corrections. My guess is that the owner of the second shop is simply unaware of the few easy steps he could take to make his shop into a top-notch facility. But that's often the difference between really good service and mediocre service. It's the little things. And losing tens of thousands of dollars each year, and possibly losing your business, is a huge price to pay for ignoring the "little things."

Here's some more real-world information: Your customers, and potential customers, are just as ruthless when it comes to judging your store. If potential customers walk through your door and are given mediocre service, often they will simply leave. They won't say a word in most cases. (I didn't say anything to the owner of the second lube shop.) If you offer mediocre service, you will have to lower your prices. And a low price incentive is a dead-end street for your store. Don't go there.

Systemize The Rule, Humanize The Exception

The way to ensure that customers get the same quality experience is to use systems or routines. You need to have a routine for all the interactions with your customers. Here is a partial list of the things I am talking about:

- How the phones are answered
- How customers are greeted
- Meeting with new prospect
- How the in-home visit is scheduled and conducted
- How installations are scheduled and conducted
- How the follow-up visit is scheduled and conducted
- The billing and payment process
- Dealing with complaints
- Handling re-orders for damaged or incorrect products

These items should be part of a system that is done the same way every time. For example, make sure that the phones are answered the same way every time. Designate specific people to answer phones and make sure they all answer the same way. Train them with a script. Also, train them how to take messages and how to handle new prospects. Streamline your accounts payable and receivable process. Do it the same way month in and month out.

This doesn't mean you can't make changes or be inventive. On the contrary, by using systems you have the freedom to step back, watch how things are running, and make *specific* changes to the system itself. But you can only make specific changes if things are already being done the same way every time.

These are very simple ideas. "Little things." But they make the difference between a great experience and a mediocre one. Professional versus amateur. Prosperous versus barely making it, or failing.

You can learn a whole lot by re-studying the differences in how both lube shops treated their customers. Develop routines for your customers and prospects so that they know they will enjoy a predictable, quality experience every single time they interact with your business.

Use Systems To Streamline Your Business—Work On Your Business, Not In It

This strategy dovetails with the previous one. Systems are a way to ensure two very important things. One, that the tasks that keep a business running are done the same way every time, with a high level of quality every time. Second, that the business will run perfectly without direct involvement of the owner. In other words, the business runs and makes a profit whether the owner is around or not. No babysitting required.

A business that has achieved this level of efficiency is also called a turnkey business. Just like you turn the key in your car's ignition and it runs by itself, you turn the key to unlock the door of a turnkey business and it runs by itself. A good example of a turnkey business that runs entirely on systems is the one I mentioned earlier: McDonald's. Have you ever noticed that a Big Mac in one town tastes exactly like a Big Mac in a town 2,000 miles away in another state? How does McDonald's ensure that Big Macs taste exactly the same no matter where you go? It's very simple. They have a system for making Big Macs. Right before my senior year in high school I spent a summer working at McDonald's, so I've seen this system first hand. Every franchise owner has a manual that describes step by step how to make a Big Mac. It tells exactly what temperature the grill should be, exactly how long to cook the patty, how much salt, how to toast the bun, how much lettuce, how much onion, how much special sauce, etc. It also explains in painstaking detail how to assemble each piece of the Big Mac. Special sauce before the lettuce, onions go on while the patty is on the grill, and so on.

When a new employee is being trained on how to make Big Macs, he or she is taught the system: how to do it by the manual, all the time, every time; no getting creative. That's how McDonald's ensures that Big Macs taste the same all over the country.

McDonald's has a system for preparing every single item on its menu. But it doesn't end with the food. You see, very few McDonald's franchises ever go broke. The McDonald's corporation has taken steps to ensure that any franchise owner, anywhere in the country, is virtually guaranteed success. How? Well, just like the systems they have created for ensuring consistency in food quality, McDonald's has also created systems that ensure consistent *operational* quality.

Every conceivable duty for running a McDonald's franchise has a written, pre-planned system. Hiring, firing, scheduling, cleaning, opening, closing, advertising, ordering supplies, personnel duties, and on and on. Everything is done the same way, all the time, everywhere.

What does this mean for the owner of a McDonald's?

First, virtually guaranteed profitability.

Second, since the owner doesn't have to work *in* his or her business, he or she can work *on* the business. Owners can concentrate on opening second and third franchises. They can examine the profitability of the store and determine what changes need to be made and assign people to make the changes. They can shape the direction of their business.

Third, he or she doesn't have to be at the business to make it work. Owners can take plenty of time off to pursue whatever activities interest them. Starting other businesses, travel, sports, family, you name it. The McDonald's store does not depend on the owner being present in order to run.

This is not the norm for most small businesses. Your typical small business is absolutely dependent upon the owner being there at all times. Why? Because the owner has placed himself in several, or many, of the key positions necessary to keep the business going. For example, the owner of a painting company does all the painting, bookkeeping, selling, and bidding. If he leaves, the company disappears. This fellow can't work *on* his business; he's too busy working *in* his business. Or the owner of a flooring dealership does the selling, booking appointments, following up with customers, ordering, and handling complaints. If he leaves, the store will cease to function. This fellow also can't work *on* his business; he's too busy working *in* his business.

What do you want out of your business?

This is a big question that only you can answer. And ultimately the answer depends upon what you want out of life. In fact, a better question to ask yourself is this: "What do I want out of life and how can my business provide it for me?" Your business is a vehicle to provide the things that you want in life, the things that have meaning to you. Your business should be engineered to revolve around your life, not your life around your business. After all, that's why you are in business for yourself instead of working a 9-5 job for somebody else, right?

Unfortunately, most floor dealers get it backward. Their lives revolve around their business instead of the other way around. This may describe you. You can't do every job in your store and expect to have any "walk-away" time. If you ever want your store to be able to run without you, you must delegate. And this is why systems are so critical.

If It's Not Written Down, It's Not A System

There are literally dozens of day-to-day tasks that are repeated by you and your staff. You should create a written system for any task regularly done in your business. Some examples:

- Your sales process (See the *Core 3* section)
- Your referral marketing process (See the *Core 3* section)
- Installation (setup, cleanup, etc.)
- Opening the store
- Closing the store
- Processing accounts payable/receivable
- Ordering materials
- Handling complaints

First, make a list of every task that needs to be done in your business. Each time you find yourself or your staff repeating a task, add it to the list. This will eventually become your company manual.

Next, take two or three of the tasks and create a written system for getting them done. Then delegate them either to an employee, or outsource them to another company. For example, all of your payroll could be outsourced to a bookkeeping company, all your mailings outsourced to a mailing house, etc. Answering phones could be delegated to an employee. After you have delegated the first few tasks, pick a few more and repeat the process.

Creating written systems for every task ensures that the task is done consistently and reliably, and most importantly gives you the freedom to think about more important things instead of worrying if a task is being done properly. It gives you the freedom to work on your business (develop marketing, spend time thinking strategically) rather than in your business (putting out fires, doing tasks that could be delegated, etc.). Delegation and training are far, far easier when you have written systems. It also makes it easier to expand or sell your business.

Creating written systems and delegating will take some time and effort up front, and you may have to move slowly depending upon what your budget will allow. But make a start. For each hour you free up from these tasks you have another hour to spend working on your business rather than in it.

Here's another way to look at it. As a business owner you are the rainmaker. You are the one responsible for marketing, creating a flow of new customers, and shaping the direction of your business. As a business owner your time is worth $500 an hour. Every time you spend an hour doing a $10 per hour task, you have lost the other $490! You would be far better off paying someone to do the $10 per hour task so you can focus on the $500 per hour activities, like creating and implementing marketing campaigns, creating affiliate relationships, etc.

TWENTY

....

IDEAL BUSINESS,
IDEAL LIFESTYLE™

FLOOR DEALER: I've been at this for 23 years, and it seems like all I do is work, work, work. I haven't taken a vacation in five years.

JIM: It sounds like you don't know the real purpose of your business.

FLOOR DEALER: What is it?

JIM: To fund and facilitate your *Ideal Lifestyle*.

The True Purpose Of Your Flooring Business

One of the principles we teach in *Flooring Success Systems* is this: The purpose of your business is to fund and facilitate your *Ideal Lifestyle*. In fact, the name of our member newsletter is *Ideal Business, Ideal Lifestyle*™.

Hundreds of dealers have been a part of the *Flooring Success Systems* program, and we've surveyed hundreds of others beyond those. A common theme when dealers first come to us is that they feel like they are working far too hard, putting in way too many hours in their business, that they don't have a life *outside* of business. Many are working 50, 60, 70 hours per week, no weekends off, and never take vacations. In fact, that's a big part of the reason dealers come to us. Yes, they want to learn the marketing strategies to increase their revenue, but that's only half of it. They also want the lifestyle. They want to build wealth. They want to be able to have some freedom and walk-away power. But they are frustrated because it seems like all they do is work, work, work.

Sound familiar?

This is why a big part of the *Flooring Success Systems* program is dedicated to helping dealers get their lives back; to helping them finally enjoy the fruits of their labors.

Why Making More Money Won't Create Freedom

Working too hard is not necessarily a lack-of-money issue. There was a dealer who was making a personal salary of $400,000 from his business, but when he first came to me he was working 60+ hours per week including weekends. He took very little time off, and didn't get to spend nearly as much time with his daughters as he wanted. He was a typical "successful slave." This situation is not uncommon. I've lost count of how many dealers who have come to me who had multi-million-dollar businesses, but were completely enslaved, stressed out, and miserable. This is because once you're making plenty of money you'll still remain enslaved to your business if you don't have systems in place to unshackle you.

My goal for this chapter is to open your eyes to what may be a new way of looking at your business. This new perspective is key in order to finally take control of your time and your life.

By the way, after a couple of months learning the strategies and principles I teach, the dealer with the $400,000 salary freed up an entire day per week without adding any more staffing. He sent me an email not long after that telling me about taking his daughters on a vacation to Disney World. Pay attention because some of the principles and strategies in this chapter are what this dealer used to make this turnaround very quickly.

Why You Started Your Own Business

We all have very personal reasons for going into business for ourselves:

- To provide a better life for our families
- To make more money
- To live in a better neighborhood
- To build a legacy for our families
- To help our kids through college
- To have the money to travel
- To support charities
- To have a nice car
- To be able to take care of my elderly parents
- Security
- To attract wealth

It's different for everyone, but the theme common to every dealer is this: They believed that going into business for themselves would be a better vehicle for achieving these things than by working for someone else. Unfortunately all too often the dreams that prompted dealers to start their dealership turn into more of a nightmare.

The Two Things Every Dealer Wants From Their Business

I've never met a dealer who went into business because they wanted to work 70 hours per week, have no life, and be perpetually stressed out. They do it because they want the things I listed above. And this basically boils down to two things: *time and money*. You need the money to be able to fund your *Ideal Lifestyle*, but you also need to be able to take time away from your business without it collapsing the minute you walk out the door.

The *Ideal Business, Ideal Lifestyle*™ Blueprint

Build Your Business Around Your Life, Not The Other Way Around

When a dealer first opens for business, or takes over an existing one, many times they are so focused on growing revenue, hiring, and wearing 20 different hats that their business takes over their life. They spend less and less time doing what has meaning, purpose, and value to them outside of business. They reach a point where they are trying to fit their life into the tiny cracks of time that are left over at the end of a 60-hour week. This is completely backward. You want to build your business around your life. You want your business to fund and facilitate your *Ideal Lifestyle*.

If you've spent years burning the candle at both ends in order to operate your business, this may sound like a crazy pipe dream. But I've helped many dealers who were stressed out, burned out, and enslaved to totally reengineer their businesses and finally achieve the dreams that inspired them to go into business for themselves in the first place. They are taking multiple vacations every year, working less than 35 hours per week, no weekends, with plenty of freedom to pursue hobbies, time with family, physical fitness, fishing, you name it. If they can do it, you can too. You just need a blueprint.

Begin With The End In Mind

When a contractor begins building a house, he doesn't just walk up to a pile of lumber and start randomly nailing things together, keeping his fingers crossed that the end result will be a livable home. The first thing he does is draw up a set of blueprints on paper. He doesn't pound a single nail until he has a crystal-clear picture of what the house is going to look like when it's completed. Then he uses the blueprint as a guide.

Unfortunately, when most dealers begin their business they don't have a clear picture of what they want it to look like when it's built. Even worse, they don't have a clear picture of how that business will enable them to live their *Ideal Lifestyle*. They're like the contractor who tries to build a house without a set of blueprints. They just start building, keeping their fingers crossed that the business will not only be successful, but that it will provide all the good things in life for which they are working so hard. Often it doesn't work out that way. Even if they manage to build a financially successful business, they've built it in such a way that they are enslaved to it.

There's too much at stake to leave achieving your *Ideal Business* and *Ideal Lifestyle* to chance. You've got to begin with the end in mind by using a blueprint. Let's take a look.

Your *Ideal Lifestyle*

The first step in achieving your *Ideal Business* and *Ideal Lifestyle* is to get a very clear picture of what you want your life to look like. Here are some questions that will help you create a very clear picture of your *Ideal Lifestyle*. Answer each of them on a blank sheet of paper. Be very, very detailed and specific. And be honest. As you answer these questions, do so with the mindset that finances and your current business situation are not an issue. In other words, answer these questions as though right now you have:

1. Plenty of time

2. Plenty of freedom

3. Plenty of money

Don't worry about "How could this be possible?" or "I could never afford it," or "I could never get away from my business long enough to do this." Part of the power of this exercise is seeing your life without all the limitations. Answer all the questions in the present tense. Don't say, "I'm going to work only three days per week, four hours per day." Instead say, "I work three days per week and only four hours per day." This makes it more real. More concrete. It brings your *Ideal Lifestyle* into the present. Let your imagination run free. I recommend doing this at a coffee shop or a park, somewhere away from all the distractions and pressures of your business.

Let's get started ...

Describe how your take care of your body, your health and well-being.

How many times a week do you walk or jog? How often do you get a massage? What kinds of food do you eat? What does your body look like? Do you study martial arts? Do you weight-lift? How often do you get out into nature for walks in the woods or along the beach, get fresh air? (Remember to answer in the present tense.)

Describe your home.

Where do you live geographically? What does your house look like? How many square feet? How many bedrooms? How large is your property? Is it in the country? Urban? Suburban? Do you have a pond? Do you live by a creek? Is your home well organized? What does your bedroom look like? Do you have a den or a library or other personal space? What does your personal space look like? (Remember to answer "<u>My</u> house ..." and "<u>My</u> property ..." Take ownership.)

Describe your relationships.

Are you married? Are you best friends with your spouse? Do you have children? What do you teach them? What are your friends like? Successful? Funny? Loyal? Spiritual? Stressed out? Negative?

What do you do for enjoyment and recreation?

You have freedom, so what do you fill the free time with? Hobbies? Writing? Fishing? Bicycling? Backpacking? Cooking? Hosting gourmet dinner parties with friends and family? Road trips? Driving from Maine to California and staying in bed and breakfasts along the way? BBQ's by the pool with all your neighbors?

What has meaning, purpose, and value to you?

Teaching Sunday school? Working in your children's youth group? Political work? Running for office? Teaching an adult literacy class? Fund-raising for a women's shelter? Beginning a trust fund for a favorite charity? Donating time, energy, money, and brain power? What kind of legacy do you want to leave behind?

What are your big, unusual, or "crazy" dreams?

These are the things that cause you to say, *Wouldn't it be neat to* … Take a month in the Caribbean? Hike in the Himalayas? Take up rock climbing? Go surfing in Hawaii? Hike the Pacific Crest Trail? Fly-fish for tarpon in Florida? Go skydiving? Spend a summer touring Europe? Live in Spain for a month? Ride my bike from Canada to Mexico to raise money for *Feed The Children*? Go to culinary school? Walk across the state to raise money for my favorite charity?

Describe what your perfect week looks like.

On another blank sheet of paper, write Monday, Tuesday, Wednesday, Thursday, Friday, Saturday, Sunday across the top. Then fill up each day, hour-by-hour, with what you'd like your ideal week to look like.

What time do you get up each morning on weekdays? Weekends?

Do you take your kids to school? Pick them up? Coach their little league team? Volunteer at your child's school?

Do you have lunch every day at your favorite restaurant with a different friend? Do you go fly-fishing every Wednesday afternoon? Golf every Thursday? Take a painting class on Tuesday evening? Band rehearsal on Wednesday evenings? Teach a literacy class on Monday evenings?

Do you spend each morning from 8 to 10 practicing martial arts? Exercising? Bike riding? Perfecting your golf game? Writing a novel? Training for a marathon?

How many hours per week do you spend working in and on your business? Eight hours per day? Six hours per day? Four days per week, Monday through Friday? Do you show up at 9:00 a.m., quit at 3:00 p.m.?

Remember to dream a little! This is *your* ideal week. Don't worry right now how you'll make it happen. Just write down exactly how you'd like it to look.

Take your time doing this. This is your life we're talking about.

Your *Ideal Business*

Next you're going to create a crystal-clear blueprint of your *Ideal Business*. As you're describing your *Ideal Business*, be sure to keep the following questions in mind:

- Will the *Ideal Business* I'm describing allow me to live the *Ideal Lifestyle* I described earlier?

- Does it give me enough time to do what has meaning, purpose, and value for me?

- Does it provide the finances I need to pay for my *Ideal Lifestyle*?

Also, don't worry about the "how" at this point. Just describe your *Ideal Business*, even if it seems a little tough to believe in right now. Again, take your time with this, and I recommend doing this exercise somewhere away from your business.

Describe your ideal work week.

How many days per month do you spend at your business? Which days? On the days you are at the store, what time do you arrive? What time do you leave?

Exactly what tasks do you do during those hours?

Think in terms of working on your business. Developing and implementing sales and marketing strategies. Strategic planning. Developing affiliate relationships. Implementing systems.

How much does your business do in gross sales each year?

Be specific.

What's your personal net income each year? (Pre-taxes)

Be specific.

How many store locations do you have?

What does your store look like?

Where is it located geographically? How many square feet of retail space? How many square feet of warehouse? Is it neat and clean? What does the sign look like? Is your office organized? Sloppy? What do the displays look like?

Describe your team.

Sales people: How many sales people? Are they neat, clean, and professional? Do your customers perceive them as Trusted Advisors or as used car salesmen? Do they look out for the needs of your customers? Are they "closers"—can they make the sale? Are they team players? Are they well paid? High turnover or low turnover? Happy to be a part of your team? Are they willing to follow the systems that give you "walk-away" power?

Installers: Are they on staff, subcontractors, or a combination? Are they neat, clean, and professional? Are they ambassadors, representing your store in a professional manner? Do they "wow" your customers with fabulous service? Can you count on them to do quality work? Are they team players? Are they well paid? High turnover or low turnover? Happy to be a part of your team? Are they willing to follow the systems that give you "walk-away" power?

Support/administrative staff: Are they neat, clean, and professional? An embarrassment? Are they ambassadors, representing your store in a professional manner? Do they "wow" your customers with fabulous service? Can you count on them to do quality work? Are they team players? Are they well paid? High turnover or low turnover? Happy to be a part of your team? Are they willing to follow the systems that give you "walk-away" power?

How does your business function when you're not around?

Do you have to "check in" with your business all the time, or do you have systems in place so it runs pretty much on its own? Does your staff continue to provide a high level of customer service and satisfaction when you're gone? Do things "fall through the cracks" — get forgotten? Or do your systems allow it to continue to function like a well-oiled machine? Are you able to stop thinking about your business while you're away?

Do your customers respect and trust you and your staff?

How much of your business comes from repeat and referral customers?

Describe any other particulars about your *Ideal Business*.

Action Plan Example

Now that you've created the blueprints for your *Ideal Business* and *Ideal Lifestyle*, let's look at an example of how you would take action on this.

Let's say that part of your *Ideal Lifestyle* blueprint is to take off every Friday to learn how to golf. You could do the following:

A) Begin to gather information on golfing. Read books and magazines. Clip out photos of beautiful golf courses where you want to play. Post the pictures on your bathroom mirror and refrigerator. Build a "dream notebook" where you keep notes, photos, price lists, etc., about golfing. Find out who the best golf pros are in your area who will train you. Visit the country club where you will be a member.

B) Determine what you would need to get "off your plate" at your store so you could take off every Friday. What would need to be delegated? How much income would you need to generate to fund membership at a country club, golf lessons, a "killer" set of clubs, etc.?

C) Write down a deadline soon enough that you are challenged, and be specific. "Friday, April 15th, will be my first Friday off. All Fridays from then on will be devoted to learning golf."

This is not an all-or-nothing proposition. It's perfectly O.K. to accomplish your goals in steps. For instance, you might not be able to take off an entire Friday immediately. That's O.K. Set an eight-week goal to take Fridays off. If you normally quit at 5:00, during your first week figure out what you have to get off your plate so you can quit by 4:00. Dedicate that extra hour to golf activities. The following week, quit by 3:00. Dedicate two hours to golf activities. Each week quit an hour earlier, clearing your plate a chunk at a time, and in eight weeks you'll have your Fridays off. This will be an extremely powerful and useful "real life" lesson in implementing the principles of systems, delegation, and walk-away power you are learning. It will also get your mind "acclimated" to creating and enjoying—and relishing—freedom.

That takes care of the "walk-away power" for Fridays. However, what if it takes six months to generate the income to pay for your membership at a country club and a top-of-the-line set of clubs? That's O.K., too. Take the Fridays off and devote the time to pursuing golf. Immediately buy a secondhand set of clubs, take lessons, practice putting in your back yard, and play on a public course. At the same time, be working toward your six-month goal of generating the income to pay for a country club membership and that "killer" set of clubs. Remember to make sure that it's a concrete, specific, written income goal. Don't say, "I'll join the country club and buy the golf clubs when I'm making enough money." That's useless. Instead write "By June 1st, I'm generating an extra $10,000 per month in gross sales. I'll join the country club and buy my killer set of dream golf clubs on June 1st."

This Dealer Is Making More While Working Less

Craig Bendele is a dealer from Florida who grew up in the business, but found there was still more to learn about being successful. Using the strategies I reveal in this book, Craig totally transformed his business and his life over a 12-month period. "Jim, I'm making more and working less!" he told me. "I used to work 'dark to dark,' including weekends. I now take weekends off, and work a lot less during the week. At the same time, my revenue is up by 50%. And my margins are at 45%. Your program has changed my life. Thank you!"

Craig's family has been in the flooring business since the mid 1950's, and in 1975 they moved to Florida and opened a store. He started out at the age of 12, sweeping the floor and mowing the lawn, moving on to warehouse management and scheduling installers. In 2004 he went into sales, and eventually took over as owner in 2011.

"I focused on the minutiae of the business like selling, closing, getting the measurements right, nylon vs. polyester," Craig said. "I hadn't thought about all the stuff that comes at you as an owner like cash flow, advertising details, or sales people showing up out of the blue."

During his first year as owner, Craig stayed on the sales floor handling sales tasks, as well as bookkeeping and all the other responsibilities. He soon found himself falling further and further behind. "A flooring manager and I used to joke that we worked dark to dark," Craig said. "The hours didn't matter, I never looked at a clock, it was just dark to dark. I worked six or seven days a week, 60-plus hours a week. My margins were low and my stress was high."

That's when Craig saw my column in *Floor Covering News*, and inquired about my coaching program. "Initially I just hoped for a new take on advertising, but I quickly realized there was much more to offer: guidance on how to truly be an owner of a business rather than just self-employed. And how to work *on* my business instead of *in* my business."

Not long after implementing the strategies he had learned, Craig had lunch with a fellow flooring dealer in his town who was new to the business. "As usual, we placed our cell phones on the table in case we got a call," Craig told me. "Mine didn't ring once, but the other guy's cell never stopped. He talked to his installers twice, the salesperson once, handling all the picky little details himself, interrupted some 10-20 times in the course of two hours. No one at my store needed me. It practically runs itself now. But my friend was totally stressed out. He couldn't even get away from his business for two hours without constant interruptions."

Within 12 months of implementing systems in his business, Craig was working far fewer hours. "I show up each day at 10:00 a.m., I leave by 5:00, and I take weekends off," Craig said. "My wife absolutely loves it. In fact, she likes it so much she's a little afraid I'll go back to working those insane hours, but I'm done with that. Even though I work five days a week, it's by choice because the business runs on systems now, even when I'm not there. I definitely work less when I want to."

Craig's revenue and margins are up, and his stress levels are down. Not only is he working less, he's making a lot more money. After less than a year of implementing these changes, his revenue was up 50% year-over-year. He has three sales people in the store, plus one commercial salesperson out on the road. He has an organizational chart, a sales manager, and an operations manager; in short, a system structure pre-built for growth. The systems he put into place means everyone knows their duties and when to do them, all the way up to Craig himself. Systems mean control, and the strategies Craig has implemented have put him in control of his business and his life.

TWENTY-ONE

....

IMPLEMENTATION

Movement Beats Meditation

Congratulations! You've made it to the end of the book. You've learned new strategies and new ways of thinking about your business that can transform your flooring dealership and change your life for the better. You've met floor dealers who have proven that by embracing new concepts, and by being willing to chuck industry norms out the window, that you can build an *Ideal Business* that funds and facilitates your *Ideal Lifestyle*.

So what should you do now?

Well, at this point you may be feeling anything from inspiration to total overwhelm, or a combination of both. You've been exposed to a ton of information, much of it probably new to you, so if you're feeling a little overwhelmed, that's understandable. It's also why I want you to make a start. Pick one thing you've learned and put it to work in your business in the next 30 days. This isn't an all-or-nothing proposition. In fact, if you try to implement everything at once you'll most likely fail.

So pick one strategy or idea you've learned, and implement it in the next month. Just one. Don't try to change the world. Just one strategy. Get it up and running in the next 30 days.

Then do it again. And again. Wash, rinse, repeat. In a year you'll have 12 new strategies operating in your business, making money for you.

You Don't Have To Go It Alone

Some dealers will take the information in this book and put it to work by themselves, and that's great. It's why I wrote it in the first place.

However, some dealers may decide that they'd like to skip reinventing the wheel and get some help putting these strategies in place. If that describes you, then I'd like to invite you to check out how my team and I can fully implement all of the Core 3 marketing systems *for you*. All the details are in the materials shipped to you with this book. Or, you can visit **YourCore3.com**.

This way you can reap the rewards without having to do the work, and without having to spend months or years of trial and error. As a business owner, the highest and best use of your time is building your business, not trying to learn, set up and run marketing systems. Especially when you can have experts handle it for you.

I look forward to coming alongside you and helping you to Beat the Boxes, and transform your business and life for the better!

Questions? Call us at 877-887-5791 or email to Support@FlooringSuccessSystems.com.

To Your Success,
Jim Augustus Armstrong
President, Flooring Success Systems

Get started beating the boxes and transforming your business and life today!

Check out the information shipped with this book, or visit YourCore3.com

ABOUT THE AUTHOR

Jim's surveys of hundreds of dealers across North America have shown that "traditional" advertising methods are failing most retailers. Realizing dealers needed help, in 2007 he founded *Flooring Success Systems*, a program which provides coaching & training for flooring dealers in the areas of sales, marketing, and motivation for total business success. His unconventional, turnkey marketing strategies empower dealers to stop wasting money on "traditional" advertising methods, and totally eliminate selling on cheap-price. Through Jim's multiple, interactive webinars each month, dealers learn to create total differentiation from their competitors, charge premium prices, and explode their profits in any market. Jim also teaches them how to make their dealerships system-dependent rather than owner-dependent, thus enabling them to achieve higher levels of success, while at the same time having a fulfilling life outside their business. A recurring theme in Jim's trainings (and the name of his coaching newsletter for dealers) is *"Ideal Business, Ideal Lifestyle™"* Many floor dealers have quickly achieved stunning success using his methods.

For information about *Flooring Success Systems* contact his office at 1-877-887-5791.

Made in the USA
Monee, IL
14 November 2020

47631195R00164